Wyrd Miniatures Presents

Malifaux

Rules Manual

DESIGNER'S NOTE

Have you ever played that game .. you know .. the one where there were great rules, but a bunch of those rules got changed? Sure they were good changes, but it left you flipping back and forth trying to find the most recent rule. Or just the most relevant rule.

Well, Malifaux was starting to become that game. But we weren't going to let you sit and do all that looking around between the books and the FAQ and the errata and your jotted notes from the house rules your friends decided on. We decided to fix it and put it all together into one complete package. Oh yeah - it's ah-maaaaz-ing! (Yes, my vibrato may be high-pitched, but it's still manly.)

This compendium is the result of our continuing efforts to support the game and make it accessible to everyone. We've clarified the rules, made the manual easier to use, and added numerous aids to make it understandable for all. And the updated style and design of the book leaves us looking good while doing it.

I love this game, and I want everyone to enjoy it. It's been a lot of hard work but the unique rules and interesting characters make the work fun. So grab your Fate by the Soulstones and play with a darn teddy bear, they're not just for 5-year-olds anymore.

Eric Johns

Eric Johns
Game Designer

CREDITS

Creator of MALIFAUX
Nathan Caroland

Creative Direction
Miniature Direction
Nathan Caroland
Eric Johns

Managing Editor
Casey Johns

Game Creation and Design
Graphic Design
Eric Johns

Rules Development Team, Editing
Dave Bowen
Drew Littell
Zafar Tejani
Dan Weber

Rules Testing
Jeremy Bernhardt
Glenn Getyina
Josh Powers
Steven Zukowski

Illustration, Logo, Concept
Melvin de Voor
Stéphane Enjoralas
Hardy Fowler
Christophe Madaru

Office Administrator
Victoria Caroland

Webmaster
Matt Kutchins

Terrain
Jeffrey Andrajack

TABLE OF CONTENTS

Intro

The Basics

The Fate Deck

The Game

Combat

Magic

Morale

Terrain & Traits

Encounters

Index

Quick Reference

INTRODUCTION

GAME OVERVIEW

Are you willing to risk your soul for a chance at great wealth and power? It's your only weapon in a world rife with monsters, necropunks, man-machine hybrids, gunslingers, and power-hungry politicos. In Malifaux, you lead your crew in the battle for control of the Breach, a dark portal to a world of limitless magic. Those who don't make it become the monsters you must destroy.

Malifaux is a character-driven 32mm tabletop miniatures game. Players lead groups, called Crews, in skirmish attacks against their opponents in the magical realm of Malifaux. Players collect, build, and paint models representing the denizens of Malifaux and pit these Crews against one another. Masters, powerful practitioners of magic, and those fighting them control these Crews.

Masters can manipulate the course of events in the world around them, and can change their own fates, through their control or theft of the powerful Soulstones in Malifaux. A Crew consists of a variety of fantastic and frightening beings, collectively known as Minions, who serve the Master as fodder in his or her machinations. In addition, Henchmen can lead specialized Crews in their Master's absence, or serve their Master directly as a member of a Crew. Masters and Henchmen are also supported by Totems, extensions of their magical abilities which increase their spellcasting range and provide additional aid in an Encounter.

How well a Crew carries out its leader's Strategy and Schemes determines whether or not it will emerge victorious in an Encounter with an enemy Crew. Strategies represent the Crew's main path to victory, while Schemes are simpler alternate routes to achieve the leader's goals.

Malifaux players use decks of cards called Fate Decks to resolve game events such as attacking and spell casting. Players can manipulate the cards they play to alter the Duel's outcome. It takes a shrewd leader to effectively utilize a Crew's resources, ensuring he or she always has ready the cards needed to Cheat Fate.

Be prepared to fight to the death because Malifaux is the end of the line!

SUMMARY OF PLAY

Before a game of Malifaux (called an Encounter) begins, players generate objectives (called Strategies) and may choose secondary objectives (called Schemes) and hire Crews. Players then deploy their Crews and let the conflict begin.

An Encounter consists of several game turns. During a turn, players draw their hands of cards (called Control Hands), which are used to change the outcome of game events such as attacks, spell casting, and so forth. Next, players determine who has the initiative, then alternate activating their models, expending Action Points to move, attack, cast spells, and so on. A turn ends after all models in play have had an opportunity to activate. Game turns continue in this fashion until the turn limit is reached. Players then total the Victory Points they earned (by completing Strategy and Schemes) to determine a winner.

WHAT YOU NEED

- Malifaux Rulebook
- 3' X 3' Playing surface
- Malifaux Models and Stat Cards
- One Fate Deck per player
- Tape measure, or other measuring tool (marked in inches)

- Terrain
- Tokens, such as glass beads, for tracking game effects
- Counters (30mm round bases) & Marker templates (base size varies)
- Blast markers (50mm round bases)

TERMS

From this point on in the rules, the first time you encounter a game term and its application, it will be listed in **bold italics** along with a corresponding entry in the index. Additionally, model Statistics, Action names, Talent names, and Spell names will be listed in **bold**.

ROUNDING

When the rules require you to halve a number, round up to the nearest whole number, unless you are halving distances; distances are not rounded.

Example: Half of 3 would be 1.5, which should be rounded up to 2.

Diagrams Key

White circles around the puppets represent the model's base.
Red areas represents an area of effect.
Green areas represent obscuring terrain.
Gray areas represent blocking terrain.
White arrows represent movement.
Blue lines represent Line of Sight.

All diagrams are show from a top down view unless otherwise noted.

Cast of Characters

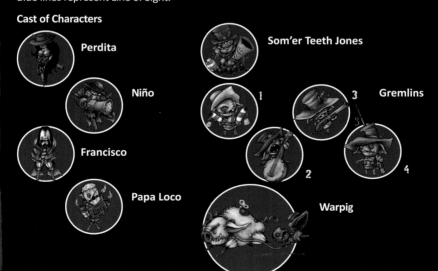

Perdita

Niño

Francisco

Papa Loco

Som'er Teeth Jones

Gremlins

1

2

3

4

Warpig

MEASURING

All distance measuring in Malifaux is done from the acting model's base edge to the affected model's nearest base edge. When measuring, a base is *within* a distance if any portion of its base is within or exactly at the indicated distance. A base is ***completely within*** a distance if the entire base is within that distance.

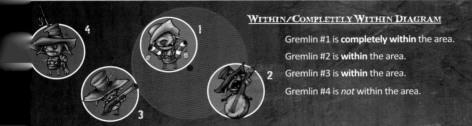

WITHIN/COMPLETELY WITHIN DIAGRAM

Gremlin #1 is **completely within** the area.

Gremlin #2 is **within** the area.

Gremlin #3 is **within** the area.

Gremlin #4 is *not* within the area.

When measuring a model's movement, measure consistently using the same reference point on the model's base. The distance any part of the base travels cannot be further than the distance permitted for that move.

There is no premeasuring in Malifaux. You must declare an Action and spend the required Action Points prior to measuring the distance required for the Action. Distances are not rounded when halving them.

> ***Example:*** *Half of 3" would remain 1.5".*

RANDOM DETERMINATION

Any time players are asked to use a randomly determined order, each player flips the top card of his or her Fate Deck. The player with the highest card chooses first, followed by the other players, in descending order. If any ties occur, the players with tied values perform a re-flip.

TIMING

Game effects follow a specific timing sequence.
- Each sentence in an effect's description must be completed before moving to the next sentence.
- If an effect causes another effect to activate while it is being resolved, pause the first effect, completely execute the newly triggered effect, and then return to the first effect at the point it was paused.
- Effects end when indicated in their descriptions. If an effect does not list an end point, it ends during the Resolve Effects Step of the Closing Phase (see p.30). Resolve ending effects in the following order:
  o At the start of a Step end first.
  o During a Step end next.
  o End of a Step end last.
  o Multiple effects that end within the same Step end simultaneously.
- Players should resolve effects occurring simultaneously in the following order:
  o Effects that <u>must</u> occur will occur before effects that <u>may</u> occur.
  o Resolve immediate effects first, then effects of the acting player, then by activation order of that player's models (p.31).
  o Any effects that are not controlled by either player, such as any terrain or environmental or Encounter effects, are resolved last and affect models simultaneously. Players with multiple models affected always resolve the effects in an order of their choosing.

The majority of effects will end in the **Closing Phase**. The ending of effects occurs in a specific order: effects that end at the start of the Closing Phase end first, followed by effects that end during the Closing Phase, and finally effects that occur at the end of the Closing Phase occur last. Within each of these steps, effects end simultaneously. If an effect does not have an end listed, it ends during the Resolve Effects step of the Closing Phase.

> **Effect Pausing Example:** The **Hangman's Knot** Spell causes "Dg 1/2/4. Push target model 4" toward this model." In this case, since the spell causes damage, if the damage kills a target it triggers any effects caused by killing that model. Once that sequence is complete, move on to pushing the target model 4" toward the caster.

> **Resolution Order Example:** The Guild's Papa Loco is targeted by Hans who is using Explosive Ammunition, which causes Blast damage. Another Guild model, Santiago, is close enough to Papa to be caught in the Blast effect. Unfortunately for Papa, the attack kills him. Papa has an ability called **Boom!** which causes him to explode when he dies. Papa Loco's Blast effect is determined first (since it was the last to occur) for any models within the blast radius, catching Santiago. Then, Hans' Ammunition Blast effect is determined for Santiago.

Math Order

Modifiers should be applied in the following order:
- First, Multiply/Divide.
- Next, Add/Subtract.

> **Math Order Example:** The Spirit characteristic halves incoming damage, while the **Armor +1** Ability reduces it by one point. If a Spirit model with **Armor +1** suffered six points of damage, the damage would be halved to three before being reduced by the **Armor** to two points.

Breaking the Rules

These rules are intended to be understood when taken as a whole. They create the framework upon which an individual model's rules are built. Because of this, **when a model's specific rule or ability contradicts these core rules, follow the specific rule rather than the core rules.** Part of the thrill of playing Malifaux is discovering interesting and entertaining options and combinations for your Crews. When the rules on two models directly contradict each other, a rule that says <u>can</u> overrides <u>may</u>, and a rule that says <u>cannot</u> will override <u>can</u>.

> **Breaking the Rules Example:** Crew hiring states that you can only hire models from your own Faction or models with the Mercenary Characteristic. The Arcanist Master, Marcus, has the **Beast Master** Ability, which allows his Crew to hire Beast models from any Faction. Marcus' specific ability takes precedence over the core Crew hiring rule.

Rule Disputes

Malifaux is designed to be fun for all players. Everyone will win and lose at times, but you should be able to enjoy the game regardless of who wins. Occasionally, you and your opponent may disagree on the clear meaning of a rule, or during the course of play you may realize an Action could not have occurred (such as bringing a third model with the Rare 2 Characteristic into play). Usually, a quick discussion of the rule or situation in question will settle the issue (such as simply removing that third model from the game). When asked, provide the information and statistics for your models honestly, accurately, and quickly.

If a solution cannot be agreed upon, each player should flip a card from his or her Fate Deck. The player with the highest card determines the outcome. Re-flip if a tie occurs. The decision made for an issue applies throughout the entire game. After the game is over, take the time to talk about and decide how you want to handle the issue in the future.

THE BASICS

WHAT MAKES A MODEL

A *model* is any number of miniatures on a single base represented by a single set of statistics. For example, the Hoarcat Pride model consists of three Hoarcat miniatures on a single 40mm base. All models in Malifaux are defined by the following information.

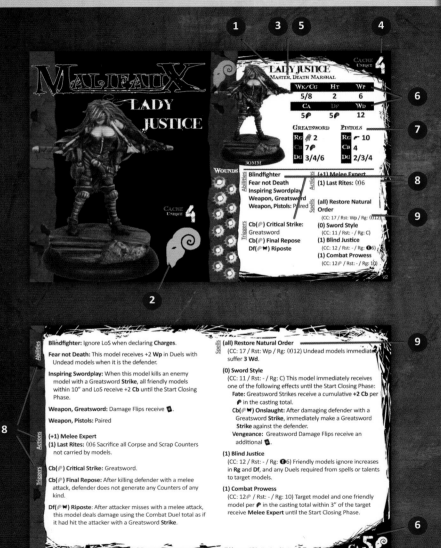

Blindfighter: Ignore LoS when declaring **Charges**.

Fear not Death: This model receives +2 **Wp** in Duels with Undead models when it is the defender.

Inspiring Swordplay: When this model kills an enemy model with a Greatsword **Strike**, all friendly models within 10" and LoS receive +2 **Cb** until the Start Closing Phase.

Weapon, Greatsword: Damage Flips receive 🔩.

Weapon, Pistols: Paired

(+1) Melee Expert
(1) Last Rites: (X)6 Sacrifice all Corpse and Scrap Counters not carried by models.

Cb(🔩) Critical Strike: Greatsword.

Cb(🔩) Final Repose: After killing defender with a melee attack, defender does not generate any Counters of any kind.

Df(🔩♥) Riposte: After attacker misses with a melee attack, this model deals damage using the Combat Duel total as if it had hit the attacker with a Greatsword **Strike**.

(all) Restore Natural Order
(CC: 17 / Rst: Wp / Rg: (X)12) Undead models immediately suffer **3 Wd**.

(0) Sword Style
(CC: 11 / Rst: - / Rg: C) This model immediately receives one of the following effects until the Start Closing Phase:
Fate: Greatsword Strikes receive a cumulative **+2 Cb** per 🔩 in the casting total.
Cb(🔩♥) Onslaught: After damaging defender with a Greatsword **Strike**, immediately make a Greatsword **Strike** against the defender.
Vengeance: Greatsword Damage Flips receive an additional 🔩.

(1) Blind Justice
(CC: 12 / Rst: - / Rg: ●6) Friendly models ignore increases in **Rg** and **Df**, and any Duels required from spells or talents to target models.

(1) Combat Prowess
(CC: 12 / Rst: - / Rg: 10) Target model and one friendly model per 🔩 in the casting total within 3" of the target receive Melee Expert until the Start Closing Phase.

1 - Name

The model's name.

2 - Faction

Which **Faction** the model belongs to. A model's Faction does not change during an Encounter, even if control of the model shifts to another player. There are five Factions in Malifaux: The Guild, Resurrectionists, Arcanists, Neverborn, and Outcasts.

3 - Type

Models in Malifaux are grouped into the following types: **Masters**, **Henchmen**, and **Minions**, which define their power level and role within the game.

Masters: Masters lead powerful Crews in pursuit of their goals.

Henchmen: A Master's aspiring lieutenant, a Henchman can lead its own Crew or join a Crew led by a Master. When leading a crew, Henchmen count as Masters for the purpose of effects, Strategies, and Schemes.

Minions: Minions are the pawns in a Master's or Henchman's schemes. They are treated with little regard and casually sacrificed in the pursuit of their leader's plans.

4 - Soulstone Cost

Generally, this number represents the number of Soulstones it costs the Crew to hire the model. Some models do not have a **Soulstone Cost**.

#: Number of Soulstones to hire

S: This model is Summoned into play (p.55) and does not have a Soulstone Cost

P: This model is Placed into play (p.38) and does not have a Soulstone Cost

–: This model is included in another model's Soulstone Cost

Masters do not cost Soulstones. Instead, they have a Soulstone Cache, which is added to a Crew's Soulstone Pool at the start of an Encounter. Also, when selected to lead a Crew, Henchmen do not cost Soulstones (p.71).

The number of a specific model a Crew can hire may also be limited. **Rare #** models are limited to the number (#) of copies of that model hired and/or in play at any time (p.71). A Crew may only have one copy of a **Unique** model hired and/or in play at any time (p.71).

5 - Characteristics

Models in Malifaux can have one or more **Characteristics**. The Characteristics listed below have additional rules associated with them. Other Characteristics have no additional associated rules but may be referenced by other game effects and abilities.

Construct: Models with the Construct Characteristic are non-living and are immune to Morale Duels (p.56).

Graverobber: When a living or Undead model is killed while one or more models with the Graverobber Characteristic are in play, replace the living or Undead model with a number of Corpse Counters equal to its base size: one for 30mm, two for 40mm, three for 50mm. These Counters can be picked up and used by models with the Graverobber Characteristic.

Henchman #: This is the Henchman Reserve. Henchmen leading Crews add the number (#) listed to their available Soulstones when hiring Crews (see Hiring, p.70). The Henchman # is also the maximum starting size of the Soulstone Pool if this model leads the Crew.

Insignificant: See Magic, p.50, Strategies, p.90, and Schemes, p.100.

Example: Models with the Construct Characteristic are not living models.

Living: All models are living models unless another Characteristic states otherwise.

Mercenary: Mercenary models can be hired by any Faction. See Hiring, p.71, for the full rules on hiring Mercenaries.

Nightmare: Models with the Nightmare Characteristic are non-living models.

Object #: Models with the Object # Characteristic are non-living models. Reduce the number of **Wd** suffered by a model with the Object characteristic by the number (#) indicated, to a minimum of 1.

Scavenger: When a model with the Construct Characteristic is killed while one or more models with the Scavenger Characteristic are in play, replace the Construct with a number of Scrap Counters equal to its base size: one for 30mm, two for 40mm, three for 50mm. These Counters can be picked up and used by models with the Scavenger Characteristic.

Soulless: Models with the Soulless Characteristic are non-living models.

Special Forces (Group Name): Up to two models with the Special Forces Characteristic may be hired per Master. A Crew cannot contain models from more than one Special Forces group. Some models lift the two model hiring limit when included in a Crew, but the limit of one Special Forces group remains (see Hire Crews, p.72).

Special Forces (Doll): In addition to the standard Special Forces rules, Zoraida may hire any number of models with this Characteristic.

Special Forces (MS&U Asset): In addition to the standard Special Forces rules, Ramos may hire any number of models with this Characteristic.

Spirit: Models with the Spirit Characteristic are non-living models that can move through other models and do not block LoS. Spirits can move over and stop on impassable terrain. Spirits are immune to Morale Duels and suffer half damage from non-magical sources. When they are killed, Spirits do not leave Counters of any type.

Totem: Models with the Totem Characteristic must be connected to a Master or Henchman when hired by a Crew or Summoned into a Crew. Each Master or Henchman can be connected to one Totem at a time unless stated otherwise. A Totem is sacrificed immediately if the Master or Henchman it is connected to is removed from the game. Totems with a Master's or Henchman's name in parenthesis can only be connected to models with that name (see Hire Crews, p.71, for the full rules on hiring and connecting Totems).

Undead: Models with the Undead Characteristic are non-living and are immune to Morale Duels (p.56).

6 - Statistics

A model's *statistics* (**stats** for short) represent its physical and mental strengths using numerical values and sometimes one or more associated suits.

Walk/Charge (Wk/Cg): Wk represents the distance, in inches, a model may cover when moving. A model may move up to its **Cg** in inches when taking the **Charge** Action. Models with a **Cg** of "—" may not take the **Charge** Action. The **Walk** and **Charge** stats cannot be reduced lower than 1 each unless an effect specifically states it is reduced to "-".

Height (Ht): How tall a model is in the game. A model's *Height* may affect Line of Sight (p.15).

Willpower (Wp): Represents a model's strength of will, determination, and self-control.

Casting (Ca): The model's ability to control the ever-present magical forces in Malifaux. Models use their **Ca** when casting spells.

Defense (Df): A model's ability to avoid being hit with a physical attack.

Wounds (Wd): The number of **Wounds** a model can suffer before being removed from the game.

7 - Weapons

A model's *Weapons* have their own stats, representing each Weapon's capabilities in the hands of that model. A Weapon's stats cannot be reduced lower than 0.

Name: The Weapon's name.

Range (Rg): A Weapon's **Rg** is the furthest effective distance, in inches, the Weapon can reach. Weapons are either melee (⫻) or ranged (➥) (see Combat, p.39).

Combat (Cb): Cb represents a model's skill with that Weapon. A model's **Cb** may include associated suits. A model uses a Weapon's **Cb** when attacking with that Weapon.

Damage (Dg): Dg indicates the Weapon's damage-inflicting potential. Depending on the quality of a hit, a Weapon can inflict Weak, Moderate, or Severe damage.

Bash

All models have access to the melee weapon **Bash** with **Rg** ⫻ **1**, **Cb 3**, and **Dg 0/1/2**, even though it is not listed on their stat cards.

Modifying Statistics

Stat modifiers are bonuses or penalties applied to a stat when resolving a situation. Stat modifiers are listed as +/- # Stat, indicating how much to add or subtract from the stat. Add bonuses (+) to stats before applying subtracting penalties (-). A stat cannot be reduced lower than 0, and any modifier that would reduce it lower reduces it to 0 instead.

8 - Talents

Models in Malifaux can possess one or more Talents. Talents are divided into four categories: *Abilities, Actions, Triggers,* and *Weapons*.

Abilities: A model's Abilities are always considered active during the game unless otherwise indicated and are applied whenever called for in the rules. This includes Abilities that grant the model additional general or specific action points (AP), such as **(+1) Fast**, or **(+2) Melee Master**. These Abilities are listed in the model's Actions entry for ease of reference. See Actions, p.32.

Actions: Any specific Actions a model can perform in addition to the general Actions outlined on p.33. This also includes any AP-granting Abilities, such as **(+1) Melee Expert**.

Triggers: Triggers can be activated when the model meets the conditions for their use (see Triggers p.26). To help players remember which stats have Triggers, those stats are highlighted in the model's Faction color on the stat card. Triggers with a suit requirement "ghosted" gray instead of black indicate that the suit requirement has been met by a suit in that stat. (**Note:** Stats which have Triggers associated with them will be colored in the model description and on the model's Stat Card.)

> **Ghosted Suit Example:** *Niño's **Cb** with his Repeating Rifle is 7🐦. He also has the **Headshot** Trigger (🐦✖) which requires he have the suits 🐦✖ in his ranged Strike Duel total to activate. Since Niño's **Cb** already includes a 🐦, the 🐦 is ghosted (🐦✖) in the Trigger's description to remind his controller the 🐦 requirement has already been met by Niño's **Cb** stat (7🐦).*

Weapons: Any Talents or special rules the Weapon possesses are listed here.

9 - Spells

Models in Malifaux may possess one or more Spells. The front of a model's stat card provides abbreviated details for each Spell, while the Spell's full details are listed on the back (see Spell Basics, p.50). Spells with a suit requirement "ghosted" gray instead of black indicate that the suit requirement has been met by the suit in that model's appropriate stat.

Model Sizes

The space a model occupies on the table is indicated by two sizes: its **Ht** and *base size*.

A model's **Ht** represents roughly how tall it is on the battlefield and allows players to compare it to the heights of other models and terrain for Line of Sight purposes. The average model **Ht** is 2, roughly representing the height of a human.

All models are mounted on one of three base sizes: small (30mm), medium (40mm), or large (50mm), as indicated in the model's description. This represents the general ground area the model occupies. A model's base size is important as Line of Sight is drawn over its base. **All models have the blocking and impassable traits, but do not provide cover** (p.58).

Friendly and Enemy Models

Because different game effects can depend on a model's current alliance with its Crew, a model will be friendly to its Crew and an enemy of opposing Crews during an Encounter.

A model is *friendly* when:
- It is under that Crew's Control
- It was hired by a Crew and is currently under that Crew's control.
- It was brought into play by a friendly model and is currently under that Crew's control.

A model is an *enemy* when:
- It is currently under another Crew's control.
- It was hired by another Crew and is currently under that Crew's control.
- It was brought into play by an enemy model and is currently under that Crew's control.

Controlling Models

The player currently in *control* of a model makes decisions for that model. All cards played for that model are played from its controller's Fate Deck and Control Hand. Any Soulstones used by the model come from its current controller's Pool. Players begin an Encounter in control of all friendly models hired by the Crew. Models able to Summon, Place, or otherwise generate additional models cannot do so while controlled by an opposing player. Those effects are ignored while the model is under an opposing player's control.

Models in Play vs. Out of Play

During an Encounter, models are either *in play* (on the table) or *out of play* (not on the table). Unless stated otherwise, only models in play can be affected by game effects and game events.

Models sometimes begin an Encounter out of play or are *removed from play* during the course of the Encounter either by being killed, sacrificed, or buried. Killed and sacrificed models are *removed from the game* completely; that is, they cannot return to play unless a specific effect allows them to do so. Buried models, on the other hand, remain *in the game* even though they are not in play and can return to play during the Encounter.

Killed: Killed models are removed from play and the game and generate any applicable Counters (e.g. living models leave Corpse Counters when killed). Models are most often killed after they have suffered enough **Wounds** to reduce their **Wd** stat to 0 (p.44), but some effects state they kill a model outright. Models killed by an effect generated by another model count as being killed by that model for Strategy and Scheme purposes.

Sacrificed: Sacrificed models are removed from play and the game when they receive a sacrificing effect. Sacrificed models do not generate Counters when removed from the table.

> *Example: A sacrificed living model does not leave Corpse Counters.*

Buried: Some models may begin an Encounter buried, or become buried by a Talent or Spell during the Encounter. While buried, a model is out of play, but still in the game and effects on the model, including **Wd** it has suffered or ongoing Spells, remain on it. A buried model unburies and returns to play when an effect allows it to do so.

> *Example: A Nightmare model buried by the Death Marshal's Pine Box could be unburied by the Dreamer's Frightening Dream spell.*

Killed and sacrificed models count as casualties for **Victory Point** purposes (see Determining a Winner, p.73); buried models do not.

Soulstones

Malifaux's Soulstones possess several amazing properties, but predictability is not one of them. Soulstones are a major commodity in Malifaux and are used in a number of ways in the Malifaux game.

Soulstone Cost

Most models cost a certain number of Soulstones to hire, as represented by their Soulstone Cost (see What Makes a Model, p.9). This cost is deducted from the number the Crew has available to hire models at the start of an Encounter (see Hire Crews, p.70). Henchmen possess a Henchman Reserve that they can add to the number of Soulstones a Crew has available for hiring models when leading the Crew. See Encounters, p.70, for full rules on hiring models.

Soulstone Cache

Instead of a Soulstone Cost, Masters possess a Soulstone Cache which is a number of Soulstones the Master holds in reserve and adds to the Crew's Soulstone Pool after the Crew has hired its models.

Soulstone Pool

During an Encounter, each Crew has a communal *Soulstone Pool*, which is determined after hiring models (see Encounters, p.72). The Crew always has a Soulstone Pool even if the number of Soulstones currently in it is 0. Players discard Soulstones from their Soulstone Pool for any models they control and apply the relevent effects. There is no need to assign Soulstones to specific models, they are in the Pool and available to the entire Crew.

Using Soulstones

When the rules allow a player or model he or she controls to use a Soulstone, that player discards one Soulstone from his or her Soulstone Pool and resolves the effect. Most of the time this will be a model with the **Use Soulstones** Ability, but on occasion a model without the ability or the player discards the Soulstone.

Models with the Use Soulstones Ability can discard a Soulstone to flip and add an additional card during Duels (see Duels, p.26), and use them to prevent and heal incoming damage (see Combat, p.48). In addition, Crews can discard a Soulstone to re-flip their Initiative Flips (see The Game, p.31).

Once a Soulstone is discarded, it is removed from the game. A Crew's Soulstone Pool should be represented by markers such as glass beads, dice, or some other method that makes it clear to all players the number of Soulstones a player's Crew has remaining. **All Masters and Henchmen have the Use Soulstones Ability unless otherwise noted in their descriptions.**

Declaring a Target

When an effect requires a *target*, the following should be determined in order:
- First, check that the item in question is in the targeting model's LoS.
- Then, check for any special situations that may allow or prevent the item to be targeted.
- Finally, check for Talents/Spells that may allow/prevent targeting.

If all of these factors allow the item to be targeted, then the model can declare that item as the target. Measure range to the target. If the target is within the effect's range and meets the above requirements, it is considered a *legal target* of the effect.

LINE OF SIGHT

A model's Line of Sight (LoS) represents what it can see on the table. When determining if a model has LoS, always remember:

- Models do not have a specific facing; they can see in any direction at any time.
- All items in play have a **base**. Models are mounted on 30mm, 40mm, or 50mm round bases (p.12). Counters are 30mm round bases, while a Marker's base size may vary (p.18). The area of table space a piece of terrain takes up is its base (see Terrain, p.58).
- LoS is not "one-way". If a model has LoS to its target without the aid of **Talents** or **Spells**, then the target has LoS to the model as well.
- Models always have LoS to themselves.

Determining LoS

When drawing LoS to an item, the line is drawn from a "top down" view over the bases rather directly to the physical bases themselves. LoS is determined using both the location of an item's base on the table as well as the item's **Ht** rather than simply whether the model can "see" the target's physical base or not. When a model attempts to draw LoS to a target, one of three conditions must exist:

- The model has **full LoS** to the target when no straight line drawn between the model and the target crosses an intervening item.
- If one or more, but not all, straight lines drawn from the model to the target cross an intervening item, then the model's LoS will be **obstructed**. The model can see its target, but the target will receive cover (see p.41) against the model's ranged attacks (⚐) if the target is within 1" of the intervening base. If the intervening object has the obscuring trait, the target receives soft cover; if it has the blocking trait, the target receives hard cover.
- If all straight lines drawn from the model to the target cross an intervening item, the model's LoS will either be obstructed, as above, or **blocked** depending on the **Ht** of the model, the target, the intervening item, and whether the intervening item has the blocking or obscuring traits (see below). A model cannot see its target if its LoS to the target is blocked.

Blocking Trait

- If all the lines drawn by the model cross any portion of an intervening base with the **blocking** trait and that base's **Ht** is equal to or greater than both the model's and target's **Ht**, then the model's **LoS to the target is blocked**.
- If the intervening base has the blocking trait and its **Ht** is less than the model's or target's **Ht**, or at least one line drawn by the model does not cross the intervening base, then the model has **partial LoS to the target**.
- A model within 1" of an intervening base with the blocking trait may ignore any cover it would provide the target.
- All non-Spirit models have the blocking trait, but do not provide cover.

Obscuring Trait

- Models can draw LoS up to 3" across an intervening base with the **obscuring** trait, but not entirely through the base.
- Models on an obscuring base can draw LoS up to 3" to other models on that base.
- If all the lines drawn by a model must be drawn across more than 3" of a base with the obscuring trait, or must be drawn entirely through the base and that base's **Ht** is equal to or greater than both the model's and target's **Ht**, then the model's **LoS to the target is blocked**.
- If LoS is drawn 3" or less across a base with the obscuring trait, or if the base's **Ht** is less than both the model's and target's **Ht**, then the model has **partial LoS to the target**. If a model draws LoS to a target that is on a base with the obscuring trait, but the line drawn does not cross the obscuring base, the target still receives soft cover.

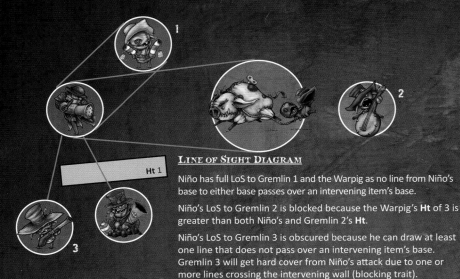

LINE OF SIGHT DIAGRAM

Niño has full LoS to Gremlin 1 and the Warpig as no line from Niño's base to either base passes over an intervening item's base.

Niño's LoS to Gremlin 2 is blocked because the Warpig's **Ht** of 3 is greater than both Niño's and Gremlin 2's **Ht**.

Niño's LoS to Gremlin 3 is obscured because he can draw at least one line that does not pass over an intervening item's base. Gremlin 3 will get hard cover from Niño's attack due to one or more lines crossing the intervening wall (blocking trait).

Niño's LoS to Som'er Teeth Jones is obstructed by the intervening **Ht** 1 wall. Since at least either Nino or Som'er is **Ht** 2, Nino has partial LoS to Som'er. Som'er will receive hard cover.

LINE OF SIGHT THROUGH OBSCURING AREAS DIAGRAM

Perdita's LoS is obstructed to Gremlin 4, but is granted partial LoS since she is drawing LoS through less than 3" of obscuring terrain. The obscuring terrain also grants Gremlin 4 soft cover from Perdita.

Perdita's LoS to Som'er Teeth Jones is blocked because she cannot draw LoS to a model completely on the other side of an obscuring base.

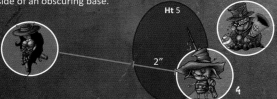

LoS and Elevations

When items are at different heights on terrain with the elevated trait, add the terrain's **Ht** to theirs when determining LoS. This type of elevated terrain (such as hills) is called *sloped* elevated terrain.

Players can choose to declare elevated terrain such as rooftops or plateaus *flat* elevated terrain rather than sloped.

Flat Elevations

Because it is difficult for a model atop a flat elevation to see targets below the following rules apply to flat elevations in addition to the standard elevated terrain rules above:
* Flat elevations have the blocking trait.
* Flat elevations have a *shadow* which extends out from their base a number of inches equal to their **Ht**.

- A model on a flat elevation cannot draw LoS to a target below while that target is completely within the elevation's shadow, unless the **Ht** of the target is greater than that of the elevation.
- A model below a flat elevation cannot draw LoS to a target on that flat elevation while the model is completely within the elevation's shadow, unless the **Ht** of the model is greater than that of the elevation.
- If LoS between a model and target passes over 1" or less of a flat elevation the model or target is standing on, the model ignores the shadow.

> *Example: A model on top of a 3" flat elevation cannot draw LoS to a model completely within 3" of the elevation.*

Sloped Elevations

Sloped elevations do not interfere with LoS the same way that flat elevations do. Models can draw LoS to targets with lower **Ht** across any amount of sloped terrain; there is no maximum distance of sloped terrain LoS can be drawn across from a model or to a target on that terrain. Models still add the sloped terrain's **Ht** to theirs when determining what items they can see over and draw LoS to. Sloped elevations have the blocking trait.

Flat Elevations and LoS Diagram

Perdita does not have LoS to Gremlin 1 because the flat elevation has the blocking trait.

Perdita does not have LoS to Gremlin 2 because its base is completely within the elevation's shadow and its **Ht** is not greater than the elevation's **Ht**.

Perdita has LoS to Gremlin 3 and Som'er Teeth Jones because neither model is completely within the elevation's shadow.

Ht 3

Side View

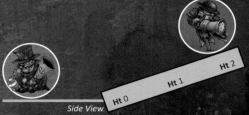

Side View   Ht 0   Ht 1   Ht 2

Sloped Elevations and LoS Diagram

Niño and Som'er Teeth can draw LoS to each other. The distance drawn across the sloped elevation is not a factor in determining LoS. However, Niño does count as standing on **Ht** 2 terrain.

LoS and Melee

A model with LoS, including partial LoS, to a target can declare melee attacks against that target. **Models do not receive cover against melee attacks.**

ATTACKS

Attacks can come from multiple sources:
- Attacks with the ⫸ icon are melee attacks, while attacks with the ⚊ icon are ranged attacks.
- Spells with a ⫸ /⚊ icon in their **Rg.**
- Spells that require a Resist Duel (see Magic, p.51).
- **Strikes** with melee/ranged Weapons (see Combat, p.39).
- Actions that inflict **Dg** or **Wd** on another model, or require an Opposed Duel.

Each of these is considered an attack, and their initiator the **attacker**. The **defender** of an attack is either the direct target when a target is required, or any models potentially affected by the attack. A model cannot attack itself unless the attack's description states that it affects friendly models.

COUNTERS

All **Counters** in Malifaux measure 30mm, have an **Ht** of 0, and have the open trait. When the rules indicate a Counter is to be placed, it must be done in such a way that it does not overlap a model's base or overlap impassable terrain. However, a Counter can overlap other Counters.

A model touching or moving over a Counter can choose to immediately gain that Counter if it is eligible to do so. A model is eligible to gain a Counter if, at the time it gains the Counter, it has the appropriate Characteristic, or possesses a Talent or Spell that uses it.

Models may carry an unlimited number of Counters during the game. Likewise, an unlimited number of Counters may be stacked together on the table in the same place. Models may only use and/or discard Counters they currently carry or that are on the table if they have the appropriate Characteristic or a Talent or Spell that requires the Counter at the time its use is indicated. Models cannot discard Counters carried by other models unless otherwise indicated in the effect's description. A model cannot use any Counters it carries while under another player's control. When a Spell calls for discarding Counters, the model removes the appropriate number of Counters from the game.

Counters a model gains must be placed where it's clear they belong to that model. A model removed from the game while carrying Counters places its Counters in a single stack where it was removed from the game.

A model cannot voluntarily drop any carried Counters or pass them to another model unless a special rule allows it to do so. Models only drop Counters they carry when they are removed from the game. If a model loses the Characteristic, Talent, or Spell that allows it to use a type of Counter it carries, it retains all of that type of Counter; it does not drop them.

Markers

Sometimes players are required to use **Markers** to indicate events, locations, or other situations that may occur during the course of an Encounter. Unless otherwise indicated, Markers are placed just like Counters and are typically 30mm round bases (but can be larger). Markers possess one or more item traits, and can be moved through or occupied, but are not considered terrain.

A Marker remains in the game as long as it takes to resolve its effects; it may remain in play for the entire Encounter. A Marker can be picked up only when permitted by a specific rule.

Tokens

Tokens represent ongoing effects currently affecting a model, and should be placed near the model. Tokens are neither Counters nor Markers and do not count as being in play for game purposes. They only track effects, and can be represented by glass beads, very small rocks, or appropriately marked 30mm round bases.

> **Example:** *A model gains two Poison Tokens. These Tokens are placed near the model to show that it is being affected by Poison, but the tokens themselves do not interact with models in play.*

The following Tokens have specific rules associated with them:

Blight Tokens: Whenever a model with one or more Blight Tokens suffers **Wd**, it suffers 1 additional **Wd**.

Burning Tokens: In the Resolve Effects Stage, a model with any number of Burning Tokens removes all Burning Tokens and either suffers 1 **Wd** or gains **Slow** (their controller's choice).

Poison Tokens: See the **Poison #** Ability, (p.116).

GAME EFFECTS

Effect is a game term referring to anything that changes a model's state. Some models are able to *ignore* or are *immune* to game effects (X). A model immune to or able to ignore X cannot be affected or modified by X when resolving the effect. Duels requiring X do not occur.

An effect can be directly referenced, such as: "**Lifer:** This model is immune to Morale Duels caused by **Terrifying** effects." Lifer indicates the model does not have to perform the Morale Duel required by **Terrifying**, regardless of its source.

A reference to an effect may have a broader application such as restricting an Ability, or only affecting or ignoring certain types of models, such as: "**Perfect Machine:** This model may choose to ignore any effect that targets Constructs." The effect here could be a Spell, a specific Weapon, an Ability, Trigger, etc. that specifically targets models with the Construct Characteristic.

Finally, multiple effects may be found in a single event. For example, a Spell may include several effects. The **Lure** Spell (spell effect) moves a model (movement effect) closer to the caster. If the model ends its move in the caster's melee range, the caster can make a melee attack against the model (melee effect).

Stacking Effects

Ongoing game effects:
- Do not stack (apply their effects cumulatively) on a model if received from Talents or Spells with the same name unless indicated otherwise in their descriptions. Ignore additional applications of the same named effect to that model.
- Do stack when listed as [name] +/-, such as Armor +1, even if they have the same name.
- Do stack when received from Talents or Spells with different names.
- Action modifiers with the same name do not stack (see p.34).

Immediate game effects:
- Occur and are applied immediately.
- Always stack with one another and ongoing effects.

> **Stacking Examples:**
> The **Hunting Dogs** Ability and **Undress** Spell are both ongoing effects that reduce **Df** by 2. Because the **Df** penalties come from two differently named Talents or Spells, they would stack and a model affected by both would suffer -4 **Df**.
>
> The Sorrow's Ability, Emotional Stress (ongoing effect), inflicts **Wd** on other models within 3" (immediate effect). The ongoing portion of the effect is applied to the Sorrow, not the models suffering the **Wd**. When a model is within 3" of more than one Sorrow, the immediate effect of Emotional Stress (the **Wd** inflicted) stacks on that model.
>
> A model with the **Armor +1** Ability in hard cover (**Armor +1**) would have **Armor +2**.

Area Effects

The three effects below are collectively referred to as **area effects**. Area effects have a **Ht** as indicated in their descriptions below and can affect anything within their area that they have LoS to. When determining if an area effect can reach models on the other side of a piece of blocking terrain, if the area effect could 'see' over or around the blocking terrain it can affect those models within its area. See p.47 for diagrams of how terrain and area effects interact.

⓵# Aura: The aura area effect represents an ongoing circular area around a target, extending from the affected base edge. All models within a number of inches equal to the aura's number(#), excluding the aura's originator, are affected for the duration indicated.

Auras move with an affected model unless otherwise indicated in the description. When a model enters an aura's area or the area moves onto the model, that model immediately receives its effects. Likewise, when the model moves out of the area or the area moves off the model, it loses the effects. Auras are infinitely high unless otherwise noted in their descriptions.

(ↆ)# Pulse: The pulse area effect represents an immediate circular area around a model, extending from the affected base edge out a number of inches equal to the pulse's number (#). It simultaneously affects all models, excluding the pulse's originator, within a number of inches equal to the pulse's number (#). Pulses are infinitely high unless otherwise noted in their descriptions.

♟ Blast: The ♟ area effect represents an immediate circular range of effect at a specific location. Place a round 50mm marker to represent the ♟ anywhere within the listed range, following any rules specific to the effect (ranged attacks must have LoS to the target, etc.). Additional ♟ can be placed so that they extend further than the effect's listed range. If the ♟ effect targets a model, at least one of the ♟ must cover a portion of the target model's base. If the effect indicates to place multiple ♟, each ♟ must be placed so that it is touching but not overlapping another ♟. All models whose bases are touched by a ♟ are affected. All blasts have a **Ht** of 3. See p.46 for how ♟ inflict damage on models and details on placing ♟s.

Each player uses a deck of cards called the *Fate Deck*, or *Deck*, to determine the success of attacks and other Actions as well as any random events in Malifaux (that's right, no pesky dice ruining your Crew's lives). Everything from determining initiative to resolving attacks, damage, and spellcasting is determined by the cards in a player's Fate Deck. Each player needs their own Deck during the game. Players only use cards from their own Fate Deck, never from another player's. Cards in a player's Fate Deck, discard pile, and cards currently revealed and in play, are collectively called *Fate Cards*.

Wyrd Miniatures produces official Malifaux decks featuring the art of Malifaux, as well as decks for use with Wyrd's *Puppet Wars* game, which can be used interchangeably for Malifaux. Players without access to Malifaux or Puppet Wars decks can play Malifaux using a standard 54 card deck of playing cards as well. See below to convert standard card suits to Malifaux's suits.

Playing Malifaux with Standard Cards

Malifaux can be played with standard card decks composed of 54 cards in 4 suits and 2 Jokers if official Malifaux decks are unavailable. The table below shows the pairings of Malifaux card suits and standard deck suits. Aces have a value of 1, and the face cards –Jacks, Queens, and Kings –have a value of 11, 12, and 13, respectively. You will also need to mark one Joker Black and one Red if they are not already marked.

Malifaux Suit	Malifaux Suit Symbol	Standard Suit & Symbol
Rams	🐏	Hearts ♥
Crows	✗	Spades ♠
Tomes	📖	Clubs ♣
Masks	🎭	Diamonds ♦

CARD VALUES & SUITS

Each card has a *value* and *suit* printed on it. When the rules refer to a card's value, they are referring to the number printed on the card, while the Fate Cards without a number but showing a suit have a value of 1. Malifaux's magic is divided into four sources, or suits: 🐏 Ram, ✗ Crow, 📖 Tome, and 🎭 Mask, that are printed on each card.

Unless the rules indicate otherwise, always include both the value and suit of a card when it is being used.

Factions and Suits

The Factions in Malifaux identify with and draw their power from one of the four sources of magic. The following table lists the magic that each Faction is most commonly associated with and the suits that represent those magical influences.

	Faction Emblem	Preferred Suit	Spheres of Influence
Guild		Rams ℰ	Buffs, Healing, Physical Damage, Willpower
Resurrectionists		Crows ✕	Armor, Death/Decay, Debuffs, Undead, Wounds
Arcanists		Tomes 📖	Constructs, Elements, Magic Damage, Magical Ability
Neverborn		Masks ⚘	Control, Deception, Defense, Speed

The Fate Deck

JOKERS

The Red and Black *Jokers* represent magic at its highest point and lowest ebb.

Red Joker – The Red Joker has a value of 14 and the suit that its controlling player nominates when it is revealed. In addition, the Red Joker may be used in Duels even when the flip has one or more a negative fate modifiers (see p.25). When making a Damage Flip with the Red Joker, it inflicts Severe damage plus an additional Damage Flip (see p.44). It also provides additional healing and damage prevention effects (see p.48).

Black Joker – The Black Joker has a value of 0 and no suit when it is revealed. The Black Joker **must be used** by a player when it is revealed, even if it is revealed with the Red Joker. Additionally, **the revealing player may not Cheat Fate further**. When making a Damage Flip with the Black Joker, it inflicts no damage (see p.44). Healing and Damage Prevention Flips with the Black Joker heal and prevent no damage (see p.48).

The Control Hand

The **Control Hand**, or **Hand**, represents how effective a Crew is at controlling the ebb and flow of magic in Malifaux. Cards in a player's Hand are called **Control Cards** and are drawn into the Hand from the Fate Deck. Control Cards can help Crews **Cheat Fate** to change the outcome of a Duel.

Maximum Control Hand Size

The maximum Control Hand size depends on the size of Encounter being played. For Scraps, the maximum number of Cards is 6; for Brawls, it is 7 (see Choose Encounter Size, p.62). During the turn, players can have more Cards in their Hands than the maximum, but they must discard down to the maximum Hand size during the Draw Phase (p.30).

Using Cards

Since the cards in Malifaux can affect the game in different ways, the rules make a distinction between **drawing**, **flipping/re-flipping**, **Cheating Fate**, and **discarding** them.

A card is considered to be in play from the time it is flipped from the Fate Deck or played from the Control Hand, until it is moved to the discard pile or back to the Hand or Deck.

Drawing: A player **draws** a Card by taking the top card from his or her Fate Deck and placing it in his or her Hand. Players can always look at these Cards as they are drawn. Cards in a Control Hand are called Control Cards.

Flipping/Re-flipping: A player **flips** a Fate Card by turning over the top card of his or her Fate Deck. A flipped Card's value and/or suit are applied immediately. Fate Cards are most often flipped to resolve game events, such as attacks or casting Spells, or to determine who has initiative each turn. **Re-flip** simply means to discard the current Fate Card in play and replace it with a new one. The number of cards a player flips may be increased due to fate modifiers (see below) applied to the flip. These modifier cards are flipped **in addition** to the initially flipped card.

Cheating Fate: Playing a Control Card from a Hand to <u>replace</u> the Fate Card in play is called **Cheating Fate**. All models can Cheat Fate but only when the rules allow them to do so. The played Control Card becomes the new Fate Card, and is placed on top of the previous Fate Card until the event is resolved. A model can Cheat Fate:

- During a Duel (p.26)
- During a Damage Flip (p.44)
- When a specific rule allows

> *Example: The description of Mortimer's Exhume Spell has him flipping a Fate Card to place a Corpse Counter nearby. It specifically states that the flip can be Cheated.*

Discarding: **Discarding** a card moves it from a player's Fate Deck, Control Hand, or from play to his or her discard pile, face up, without applying its value or suit.

The Discard Pile

Players should keep their **discard piles** near their Fate Decks for easy access. All Cards in the discard pile should be face up, with the most recently discarded Card on the top. Players may not look through any discard piles, neither their own nor another player's, and cannot change the order of Cards in their discard pile.

After a game event in which a player used Cards is completed, immediately move those Cards to that player's discard pile, face up, in the order they were used with the last Card used on the top. If the event was a Duel, the Cards used during the Duel are placed into the discard pile in the same way as above when the Duel is completed. Until then, they should be stacked in such a way that the only Card(s) visible are the Cards that are currently active.

Running Out of Fate Cards

When a player needs to draw or flip a Fate Card and his or her Fate Deck is empty, the player picks up his or her discard pile, **re-shuffles** the Cards, and places them face down. This starts a new Fate Deck. Cards currently in play, or that currently reside in a Control Hand, may not be shuffled into the new Fate Deck. Players should always give their opponents an opportunity to cut the Deck after shuffling it for any reason.

TWISTING FATE

Normally, players flip one card when a Card flip is required. **Fate modifiers** increase the number of cards flipped when resolving a game event and are indicated by a ⊞ for a positive fate modifier and a ⊟ for a negative fate modifier.

When a model is affected by one or more fate modifiers, total up the number of ⊞ (positive) modifiers, then subtract the total number of ⊟ (negative) modifiers to see how many **additional** cards to flip. The total number of additional cards flipped due to fate modifiers (whether positive or negative) can never be more than three, regardless of how many modifiers are applied. **Remember: fate modifiers are cards flipped in addition to the initial card flipped.**

After totaling up fate modifiers:

- 0 (no ⊞ or ⊟ fate modifiers): Flip one Fate Card; this is the standard number of Cards flipped during an event.
- ⊞, ⊞⊞, or ⊞⊞⊞ (one, two, or three positive fate modifiers): Flip **one additional** Fate Card per ⊞. Choose one Card to use and place that Card on top of any other flipped Cards.
- ⊟, ⊟⊟, or ⊟⊟⊟ (one, two, or three negative fate modifiers): Flip **one additional** Fate Card per ⊟. Keep the lowest value Card to use and place that Card on top of any other flipped Cards. If the lowest value is tied between two Cards, the controlling player can choose which Card to keep. **The player cannot Cheat Fate for this flip.**

> **Twisting Fate Example:** A model receives ⊞ to its Damage Flips. It **Charges** an enemy model (another ⊞ modifier). The enemy model has the **Hard to Wound 1** Ability, which modifies Damage Flips against it by ⊟. The total modifier to the charging model's Damage Flip would be ⊞ (⊞ + ⊞ - ⊟ = ⊞). When the model flips for damage, it flips two cards and chooses which card to keep and use.

Jokers and Twisting Fate

Regardless of the number of Cards flipped, a player must choose to keep and use the Black Joker if it is flipped, even if the Red Joker is also flipped. If the Red Joker is part of a negative modifier flip, it may be still be used, even if it is not the lowest value card.

DUELS

Duels are used to resolve most events during a game of Malifaux. There are two types of Duels: *simple* and **opposed**. A simple Duel is a Duel against a predefined **target number** (TN); an opposed Duel is a Duel against another model's total. During a Duel, each model involved has an opportunity to affect the Duel's outcome by Cheating Fate.

Triggers

Some models possess one or more **Triggers** which can be used during Duels. A Trigger consists of the stat it is connected to, as well as the suit(s) a model needs in its Duel total for its use. When the model is using the stat indicated in the Trigger in a Duel and has the suit(s) needed in its total, it can declare it is using the Trigger, applying the Trigger's effects as indicated in its description. A model can only declare it is using one Trigger during a Duel, regardless of the number of Triggers it possesses. If a Trigger allows the model to take additional Actions, those Actions do not cost AP (see Actions, p.32) to use. Paralyzed models may not declare Triggers. The effects of a Trigger are limited to the Action it is activated with. Additional models are not affected by the Trigger unless it is stated otherwise in its description.

> *Example: The **Critical Strike** Trigger inflicts additional **Dg** to the target of an attack. If that attack also inflicted 🏆 damage, models touched by the 🏆 would not suffer the additional damage from **Critical Strike**.*

PERFORMING A SIMPLE DUEL

A simple Duel pits the model against a set target number (TN) and is listed as the stat vs. the TN (Stat → TN).

If a game effect requiring a simple Duel affects multiple models, the affected models perform the Duel in an order of their Controller's choosing. When more than one Controller has models affected, use the turn's activation order (p.31) to determine which Controller performs their models' Duels first.

1. Flip for Starting Duel Total. The model flips one Fate Card + one Fate Card per fate modifier (🃏 or ⊟). If the flip had a positive modifier (one or more 🃏), then the model chooses which of the flipped Cards to keep. If the flip had a negative modifier (one or more ⊟), then the model must choose the lowest value Card. If one of the flipped Cards was the Red Joker, the player may choose to keep it regardless of fate modifier. If one of the flipped Cards was the Black Joker, the player <u>**must**</u> keep it regardless of any other Card flipped, including the Red Joker. Place the chosen Card on top of any other flipped Cards.

Starting Duel total = Fate Card's value and suit + stat value and any suits + applicable modifiers.

- If the starting Duel total is equal to or greater than the TN and includes at least one of each suit in the TN, the model is winning the Duel. (**Success**)
- If the starting total is less than the TN and/or is missing one or more of the suits in the TN, the model is losing the Duel. (**Failure**)

2. Change Starting Total or Pass. The model may use either or both options below, in the order listed, but can use each option only once. A model may choose not to use either option and move on to Step 3 instead.

- **Cheat Fate**: The model performing the Duel may replace the flipped Fate Card with a Control Card from its Control Hand. Place the Control Card on top of any other Cards the model has in play. **A model cannot Cheat Fate if it has a negative fate modifier or its current Fate Card is the Black Joker.**
- **Use Soulstones**: If the model has the **Use Soulstones** Ability, it may discard a Soulstone to flip a second Fate Card and add its value and suit to the Duel total. Place this card next to the Fate Card in play. If the Black Joker is flipped, it adds nothing to the total; it does not replace it. **A model can Use Soulstones even if it has a negative fate modifier or its current Fate Card is the Black Joker.**

Performing a Duel

1. Flip for Starting Duel Total.
2. Change Starting Total or Pass.
   a. Cheat Fate
   b. Use Soulstones
3. Determine Final Duel Total.
4. Declare Trigger.
5. Determine Success.
6. Apply Duel Results.

3. Determine Final Duel Total. This is determined after the model has had an opportunity to change its starting Duel total.

Final Duel total = Fate Card value and suit (original or replacement from Cheating Fate) + stat value and any suits + applicable modifiers + value and suit of any Fate Card from Using Soulstones.

4. Declare Trigger. The model may now declare that it is using one Trigger that it has met the suit requirements for. The Trigger's description will indicate when its effects are applied.

5. Determine Success.

- If the model's final Duel total is equal to or greater than the TN and includes at least one of each suit in the TN, the model has won the Duel. (**Success**)
- Otherwise, the model has lost the Duel. (**Failure**)

6. Apply Duel Results. The results of winning or losing the Duel are applied as indicated by the Duel.

Simple Duel Example

*Lady Justice wants to **Charge** Teddy, who has the **Terrifying → 13** Ability. Before she can do so, Lady Justice must win a simple Duel with a TN of 13.*

1. Model Flips for Starting Duel Total: *Lady Justice flips the 4♥, adding her 6 **Wp** for a total of 10♥. Right now her total is less than the Duel's TN of 13, so she is losing the Duel.*

2. Model Chooses Whether to Change Starting Totals or Pass: *Lady Justice's controller happens to be holding the 9♣ in his Control Hand and decides to Cheat Fate by using this card to replace the 4♥. Lady Justice does have the **Use Soulstones** Ability, but decides to not use it to add another Fate Card to her total.*

3. Model Determines Final Duel Total: *Lady Justice's final total is now 9♣ + Wp 6 = 15♣, which is equal to or greater than the TN of 13 needed to overcome Teddy's **Terrifying** Ability.*

4. Model Declares Trigger: *Lady Justice does not have a Trigger that uses her Wp stat that she could declare so she skips this step.*

5. Model Determines Success: *Since Lady Justice's final total (15♣) is equal to or greater than the TN (13), she has won the Duel.*

6. Model Applies Duel Results: *A model winning a **Terrifying** Duel ignores the effects of Terrifying. This allows Lady Justice to continue her charge at Teddy and beat the stuffing out of him.*

Resolving an Opposed Duel

An opposed Duel pits the acting model's stat against the opposing models' stats (**Acting Model's Stat → Defending Model's Stat**). It may not always be clear which model is the acting or defending model in an opposed Duel. When in doubt, remember that any time targeting is mentioned, the target is automatically the defender. If no target is required, or there is no acting model at the time, the acting model should be the model controlled by the current acting player, or the next player in the turn's activation order (p.31).

1. Flip for Starting Duel Totals. Each model flips one Fate Card + one Fate Card for each fate card modifier (🦅 or ⊟) applied to its respective flips. If the flips had a positive modifier (one or more 🦅), then the model chooses which of the flipped Cards to keep. If the flip had a negative modifier (one or more ⊟), then the model must choose the lowest value Card. If one of the flipped Cards was the Red Joker, the player may choose to keep it regardless of fate modifier. If one of the flipped Cards was the Black Joker, the player **must** keep it regardless of any other Card flipped, including the Red Joker. Place the chosen Card on top of any other flipped Cards. In the case of both models having fate modifiers, the acting model must choose its card first.

Starting Duel total = Fate Card value and suit + stat value and suit + applicable modifiers.

Compare the models' starting totals. The model with the higher total is winning the Duel.

- If the acting model has a higher total, or the totals are tied, it is winning the Duel. (**Success**)
- The acting model is losing the Duel if its total is less than the defending model's total. (**Failure**)

2. Change Starting Totals or Pass. Starting with the losing model, each model may use either or both options below, in the order listed, but can use each option only once. A model may choose to pass and not use either option. If both models pass changing their totals, move on to Step 3 below.

- **Cheat Fate**: The model may replace the flipped Fate Card with a Control Card from its Control Hand. Place the Control Card on top of any other Cards the model has in play. **A model cannot Cheat Fate if it has a negative fate modifier or its current Fate Card is the Black Joker.**
- **Use Soulstones**: If the model has the **Use Soulstones** ability, it may discard a Soulstone to flip a second Fate Card and add its value and suit to the Duel total. Place this card next to the Fate Card in play. If the Black Joker is flipped, it adds nothing to the total; it does not replace it. **A model can Use Soulstones even if it has a negative fate modifier or its current Fate Card is the Black Joker.**

3. Determine Final Duel Totals. This is determined after both models have had an opportunity to change their starting Duel totals.

Final Duel totals = Fate Card value and suit (original or replacement from Cheating Fate) + stat value and any suits + applicable modifiers + value and suit of any Fate Card from Using Soulstones.

4. Declare Trigger. Starting with the model with the lower total, or the defending model if the totals are tied, each model may now declare one Trigger that it has met the suit requirements for. The Trigger's description will indicate when its effects are applied.

5. Determine Success.

- If the acting model's final Duel total is equal to or greater than the defending model's final Duel total, it wins the Duel, and the defending model loses the Duel. (**Success**)
- Otherwise, the acting model has lost the Duel and the defending model has won. (**Failure**)

6. Apply Duel Results. The results of winning or losing the Duel are applied to each model as indicated in the Duel's description.

Note

The model currently taking Action is referred to as the *acting model, attacking model,* or *attacker.* The model responding to the Action is referred to as the *target model, defending model,* or *defender.*

Opposed Duel Example

Candy wants to **Pacify** a Guild Guard (both have **Wp** 5). **Pacify** requires an opposed Wp → Wp Duel.

1. Models Flip for Starting Duel Totals. Candy and the Guild Guard each flip a Fate Card. Candy flips a 7✕ and the Guild Guard flips a 10▦. When we compare the totals, Candy's 12✕ to the Guild Guard's 15▦, we see that Candy is currently losing the Duel.

2. Models Change Starting Totals or Pass. As Candy is losing the Duel, she has to Cheat Fate or pass first. She doesn't have the **Use Soulstones** Ability so she cannot add a Fate Card. She chooses to replace her current Fate Card with a 13✕. The Guild Guard passes.

3. Models Determine Final Duel Totals. Candy's final total is now 18✕, while the Guild Guard's remains 15▦.

4. Models Declare Triggers. Neither model has a trigger it can activate, so they both pass.

5. Determine Success. Candy wins the Duel since her total is higher than the Guild Guard's.

6. Apply Duel Results. Candy now applies the effects of **Pacify** to the Guild Guard.

DETERMINING DUEL TOTAL DIAGRAM

The following is how you would determe a Duel total when a player Cheats Fate and chooses to use a Soulstone during a simple **Wp** → **17** Duel. The model's statistic is 4♥; it flips a 7♠ but decides to Cheat Fate, replacing it with a 12♥ from the Control Hand. The player decides to use a Soulstone to draw a Card, in this case a 4✕, and adds it to the total. The final Duel total is 20♥♥✕, and the model succeeds in the simple Duel.

WP Statistic	Card Flipped is Replaced by Cheating Fate with a Card from the player's hand	Use a Soulstone to Flip and add one additional Card	Duel Total

4♥ +  + = 20♥♥✕

The Turn

A Malifaux Encounter consists of a number of turns in which players alternate activating models until both sides have activated their entire Crew.

Each *turn* is broken into 3 *phases* – *Draw*, *Activation*, and *Closing* – in which each phase is composed of an ordered sequence of required steps. Each phase and its steps occur in the specific order outlined below during every turn. Once a turn's Closing Phase is completed, the next turn begins. Effects ending during Steps do so as indicated in Timing, p.6.

Turn Sequence

1) **Draw Phase**
   A. Start Draw Phase Step
   B. Discard Control Cards Step
   C. Draw Control Cards Step
   D. End Draw Phase Step
2) **Activation Phase**
   A. Start Activation Phase Step
   B. Flip for Initiative Step
   C. Alternating Activations Step
   D. End Activation Phase Step
3) **Closing Phase**
   A. Start Closing Phase Step
   B. Resolve Effects Step
   C. Shuffle Fate Decks Step
   D. End Closing Phase Step

1) Draw Phase

Each step in the Draw Phase is taken using the previous turn's activation order. On the first turn, skip steps A and B and start with step C of the Draw Phase.

A. Start Draw Phase

Any effects which indicate a start, occur, or end during the Start Draw Phase, respectively start, occur, or end.

B. Discard Control Cards

Players may discard any number of Control Cards from their Control Hands at this time.

C. Draw Control Cards

Players draw Control Cards until they reach the maximum Hand size for the Encounter size (6 for Scrap, 7 for Brawl) they are playing. If a player is already holding the maximum number of Cards, that player does not draw any cards. If a player has more Cards in his or her hand than the maximum, that player does not draw any cards and must discard Cards until he or she has no more than the maximum number of cards allowed in his or her Hand.

If this is the first turn, players simultaneously draw their Hands.

Game Size	Maximum Hand Size
Scrap	6
Brawl	7

D. End Draw Phase

Any effects which indicate a start, occur, or end during the End Draw Phase, respectively start, occur, or end.

2) Activation Phase

A. Start Activation Phase

Any effects which indicate a start, occur, or end in the Start Activation Phase, respectively start, occur, or end. If this is the first turn of the game, randomly determine which player resolves his or her effects first, then continue in the randomly determined order.

B. Flip for Initiative Step

Players now flip a Fate Card and compare the values; this is known as the *Initiative Flip*. If the Fate Card values are tied, no player has the option to use a Soulstone. All players re-flip.

If the Fate Card values are not tied, the player with the lowest Fate Card has the option to discard a Soulstone and re-flip the Fate Card. Once that player has made and acted on the choice to re-flip, the opponent with the next lowest total may then choose to discard a Soulstone and re-flip. The order to discard a Soulstone to re-flip the Fate Card is resolved in order from the player with the lowest Fate Card value to the player with the highest Fate Card value, until all players have had the option to re-flip. Each player has the option to reflip, even if they do not have any models with the **Use Soulstones** ability left in play.

After all players have had an opportunity to re-flip once, if any of the Fate Card values are tied, the players with tied values repeat the Flip for Initiative step from the beginning. If the Flip for Initiative step is repeated, all players again have the option to discard one Soulstone and re-flip once. The player with the highest value has *Initiative* for this turn and activates a model first.

C. Alternating Activations Step

Beginning with the first player, each player, from highest to lowest Initiative value, activates one model and uses all of its action points for the turn. This player order for activating models is called the turn's *activation order*. Players continue activating using the turn's activation order until all of their models in play have activated at least once during the turn.

If a player has models to activate, that player must activate one when it is his or her turn to do so. If a model is unable to take any Actions when it is activated, that model's controller simply passes activation to the next player in the activation order. If a player has no models left to activate but other players do, that player's activation turn is skipped. Each model may activate only once during a turn unless otherwise indicated by a model's ability. Turning your models' stat cards or marking them with glass beads or other Counters after they have activated is a good way to keep track of which models still need to activate.

D. End Activation Phase Step

Any effects which indicate a start, occur, or end in the End Activation Phase, respectively start, occur, or end.

Multiple Activations

When an effect allows a player to activate two or more models simultaneously, that player first states all of the models he or she is activating. Next, the player selects the first model in the group and activates it as normal, completing its entire activation before moving on to the next model, and so on, until all of the models acting simultaneously have completed their activations. Once the player has completed all of the activations, activation passes to the next player in activation order.

A model allowed to activate immediately by an effect does so before any other model activates, but after the current model's activation ends.

3) Closing Phase

The Closing Phase occurs after all models in play have been activated. Each step in the Closing Phase is taken in activation order.

A. Start Closing Phase Step

Any effects which indicate a start, occur, or end in the Start Closing Phase, respectively start, occur, or end.

B. Resolve Effects Step

All Action and Spell effects which do not indicate a duration end during this step.

C. Shuffle Fate Decks Step

Players collect their discard piles and shuffle them back into their Fate Decks. Cards in a player's hand are kept and not shuffled back into the Fate Deck.

D. End Closing Phase Step

Any effects which indicate a start, occur, or end in the End Closing Phase, respectively start, occur, or end. Any player with cards in his or her discard pile at the end of this Phase must reshuffle his or her Deck and discard as in C. above.

Actions

Action Basics

Each model receives two (2) *general action points (AP)* at the start of its activation. Some Triggers, Abilities, and game effects may increase or decrease the number of AP a model receives during its activation. In addition:

- Action names appear in **Bold**, preceded in parentheses by the number of AP the model must spend to take the Action. If the model does not have the required number of AP available, it cannot take the Action. Unless stated otherwise, a model can take the same Action any number of times as long as it has the AP to spend.

  Action Example: (1) Walk, (1) Strike, or (2) Charge.

- Some Actions require zero AP, indicated by **(0)** preceding the Action. A model may only use one **(0)** Action during its activation. A model may only take **(0)** Actions during its own activation.
- If a model performs an **(all)** Action, it is the only Action that model may take during its activation, including **(0)** Actions. A model cannot take an **(all)** and a **(0)** Action during a single activation. Additional Actions generated from Triggers may be used as normal when a model performs an **(all)** Action.
- A model may not have any AP remaining at the end of its activation. If any AP are remaining, the model is considered to have taken the **Pass** Action with those AP.

  (All) Action Example: Lady Justice wants to cast (all) Restore Natural Order. If she has taken any Actions during her activation, including casting her (0) AP cost Sword Style spell, she could not cast Restore Natural Order. After casting and resolving Restore Natural Order, her activation ends.

GENERAL ACTIONS

General Actions are common game Actions available to all models, unless otherwise indicated in the Action's description. Some general Actions are listed below while others are outlined in the appropriate chapters throughout this book (e.g. general combat Actions are listed in the Combat chapter). A model can spend general AP or the appropriate specific AP to take a general Action.

General Actions

(1) Heal: Models with **Use Soulstone** only. Discard 1 Soulstone. This model makes a Healing Flip (p.48).

(#) Interact: This model spends the indicated number of Actions to Interact with the game table or terrain piece.

> *Example: Picking up a bag of Soulstones in a story scenario is a (1) Interact Action.*

(1) Pass: This model does nothing for this Action.

(all) Scavenge: Scavengers Only. This model gains 1 Scrap Counter.

SPECIFIC ACTIONS

Many Actions are only available to certain models and are listed in the model's description. These *specific Actions* list their AP cost before the Action name just like general Actions. Regardless of their source, specific Actions do not stack.

Specific Action Points

Some Abilities grant a model additional AP for specific Actions. These *specific AP* Abilities list the additional AP granted as a (+ or sometimes -#) in front of the Ability's name: **(+1) Melee Expert**, for example. These specific AP can be spent only on the Actions indicated in the description, and may not be combined with other AP, either general or specific, unless the Ability permits. Specific AP are added to a model's available AP at the beginning of its activation, or when noted in the Ability's description and can be spent along with general AP in whatever order its controller chooses. A model does not have to use a Pass Action for any unused specific AP. Unused specific AP are lost at the end of the model's activation. Regardless of their source, specific AP with the same name do not stack.

> *Specific Actions Example:*
> *(2) Flurry: This model immediately makes up to 3 melee Strikes against a single model. Madame Sybelle spends 2 general AP to perform Flurry and immediately receives 3 specific AP to use only for 3 Strike Actions against a single model. Madame Sybelle cannot combine two of the 3 Actions to Focus because Flurry requires the AP to be used specifically on melee Strikes.*

> *(+1) Melee Expert: This model can make an additional melee Strike during its activation. Baby Kade has (+1) Melee Expert, so he receives 3 AP at the start of his activation; 2 general AP plus 1 specific Melee Expert AP that can only be spent on a melee Strike. If Baby Kade does not want to, or does not have the opportunity to perform a melee Strike during his activation, the 1 AP from Melee Expert is lost at the end of his activation. He does not have to use a Pass Action.*

ACTION MODIFIERS

The four game Abilities that increase or decrease the number of general AP a model receives during its activation are collectively called **Action modifiers**. Action modifiers with the same name do not stack.

- **(+1) Fast:** This model receives 1 additional general AP during its current or next activation, whichever comes first.
- **(-1) Slow:** This model forfeits 1 general AP during its current or next activation, whichever comes first.

If a model affected by **Fast** gains **Slow**, or vice versa, the two cancel each other out and both effects are removed. A model is not affected by both **Fast** and **Slow** at the same time.

- **Paralyzed:** A model gaining **Paralyzed** during its activation loses any remaining AP and its activation immediately ends. If the model gains **Paralyzed** outside of its activation, it forfeits its next activation. While **Paralyzed,** a model has no melee range, cannot take any type of Action, cannot activate Triggers, and cannot react to disengaging models. A **Paralyzed** model does not make a fall back move when it loses a Morale Duel, but does rally as normal (Morale, p.56).
- **Reactivate:** This model may activate a second time this turn during the normal activation sequence. A model may only activate a second time through **Reactivate** once per turn.

If a model affected by **Reactivate** gains **Paralyzed**, or vice versa, the two cancel each other out. A model is not affected by both **Reactivate** and **Paralyzed** at the same time.

> *Action Modifier Examples: Lilith has **(+1) Fast** and Mortimer casts **(-1) Slow** twice on Lilith. The first **Slow** cancels Lilith's **Fast**, and the second Slow nets Lilith -1 AP on her next activation. Perdita Ortega has **(+1) Fast** and the Student of Conflict Totem uses an Ability to give **(+1) Fast** to her. Since Action modifiers of the same name do not stack, Perdita only receives **(+1) Fast**, not **(+2) Fast**.*

> *Combining Actions Modifiers Example: Viktoria has **(+1) Melee Expert** and is affected by a spell that causes **Slow**. At the start of her activation, she will receive 1 general AP and 1 specific AP for melee **Strikes**. Before the start of her activation, she receives **Fast**. Since Fast negates **Slow**, Viktoria now receives her usual 2 general AP, as as well as a third AP for use on melee **Strikes**.*

MOVEMENT

During the course of an Encounter, models will change their positions on the table through one of the following types of effects: **movement effects** (see Movement Effects below), **placement effects** (see Placement Effects below), or **summoning effects** (see Summoning, p.55).

When a player is allowed to control an enemy model's movement due to a game effect such as a Spell, that player can move that model in any legal direction he or she chooses, including walking it off a cliff or into bubbling lava if such a move would be legal for the model to make.

Movement Effects

When measuring a model's movement, measure consistently using the same point on the model's base. A model's base is not allowed to pass over another model's base as it moves nor is a model allowed to end its move on top of another model's base. If a model's base does not fit through a gap between model bases and/or terrain, the model must find an alternate path or stop its movement at the point where it can no longer pass. The distance a model can move may be affected by terrain (p.58).

Any time the model takes the **Walk**, **Charge**, or **Jump** Actions, is moved using its **Walk/Charge** stat, is Pushed, or falls back (see Falling Back, p.57), it is being affected by a *movement effect*.

Models forced to move:
- **Toward / away from** something (another model, a specific point, table edge, etc.) must move by the shortest route. A model moving in this manner cannot end the movement further (for toward) or closer (for away from) from the thing than it began. However, the model may move in such a way as to avoid any terrain or impassable items.
- **Directly toward / away from** something move as far as the effect requires in a straight line. Models will stop this move if they come into contact with other intervening models or terrain they could not move through or over.

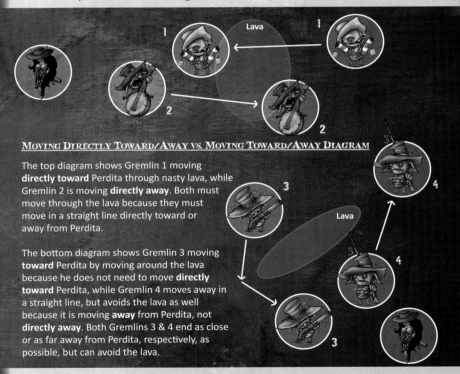

MOVING DIRECTLY TOWARD/AWAY VS. MOVING TOWARD/AWAY DIAGRAM

The top diagram shows Gremlin 1 moving **directly toward** Perdita through nasty lava, while Gremlin 2 is moving **directly away**. Both must move through the lava because they must move in a straight line directly toward or away from Perdita.

The bottom diagram shows Gremlin 3 moving **toward** Perdita by moving around the lava because he does not need to move **directly toward** Perdita, while Gremlin 4 moves away in a straight line, but avoids the lava as well because it is moving **away** from Perdita, not **directly away**. Both Gremlins 3 & 4 end as close or as far away from Perdita, respectively, as possible, but can avoid the lava.

Climbing

A model can climb any vertical surface with the climbable trait at any time when moving (p.58). The model moves 1 **Ht** for every 2" of movement it spends. If the model ends its activation short of the top or bottom, mark the model's height with a marker indicating how high it is.

Movement Penalties

Movement penalties may apply when a model uses a movement effect. All penalties to movement are cumulative, but a model's **Wk/Cg** cannot be reduced lower than 1/1, unless an effect specifically reduces the stat to "-" (Terrain, p.58).

Terrain Type	Penalty
Severe	Movement through severe terrain costs double the distance moved.
Impassable	Cannot enter
Hazardous	Suffer damage (p.59)
Climbable	Movement up or down climbable terrain costs 2" per 1 **Ht**.

General Movement Actions

(1) Walk: This model moves up to its **Wk** in inches. This may be in any direction and does not need to be in a straight line. A model may **Walk** into melee combat if it chooses.

(2) Charge: This model may take the **Charge** Action if it has a target model within its LoS, which is not already in its melee range. The charging model must move up to its **Cg** in a straight line toward the target, making every effort to end the move with the target in melee range. The model must obey the normal rules for movement including movement penalties and disengaging **Strikes.** At the end of the **Charge** move, if the target is in melee range, the model immediately makes a melee **Strike** with one of its melee Weapons and receives 🎴 on its Damage Flip for that attack. If the target of the Charge is out of melee range at the end of the model's move, the **Charge** Action ends immediately.

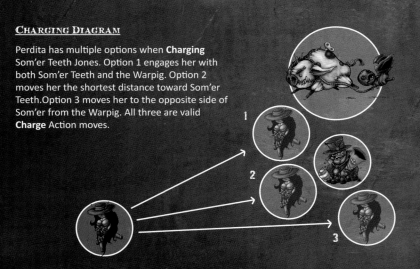

CHARGING DIAGRAM

Perdita has multiple options when **Charging** Som'er Teeth Jones. Option 1 engages her with both Som'er Teeth and the Warpig. Option 2 moves her the shortest distance toward Som'er Teeth. Option 3 moves her to the opposite side of Som'er from the Warpig. All three are valid **Charge** Action moves.

(2) Jump: The model can either move 1/2 of its **Wk** distance horizontally and can move over gaps, or the model can move up to 1/2 of its **Wk** distance from a higher elevation to a lower one, or vice versa, without suffering damage.

Pushes

When a game effect *Pushes* a model, it is moved the distance indicated by the effect causing the Push. Pushes are move effects and are affected by movement penalties, but do not generate disengaging **Strikes**.

When a game effect indicates that a model should be Pushed to within a specific distance of something, it is Pushed, ignoring Movement Penalties, to that specific distance of something. If a game effect indicates that a model should be Pushed to completely within a specific distance of something, the model is Pushed, ignoring Movement Penalties, until the entire base is within that distance. If the entire base does not fit within that distance, the Push cannot be made.

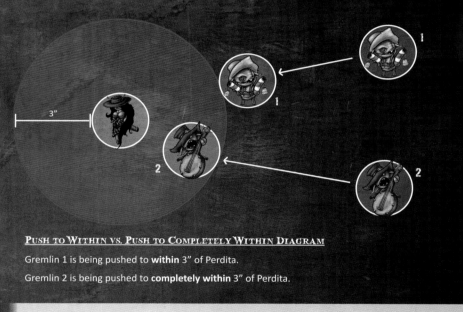

<u>**PUSH TO WITHIN VS. PUSH TO COMPLETELY WITHIN DIAGRAM**</u>

Gremlin 1 is being pushed to **within** 3" of Perdita.

Gremlin 2 is being pushed to **completely within** 3" of Perdita.

Flying Models

Models with the **Flight** Ability move over terrain without penalty and over other models but cannot end their movement in or on impassable terrain or another model's base.

Models with the **Float** Ability move over terrain without penalty and over other models, and can end their movement over impassable terrain but cannot end their movement over another model's base.

Models with the **Flight** or **Float** Ability ignore enemy models' disengaging **Strikes** when moving except for disengaging **Strikes** from models whose melee ranges they began the movement within. These models also ignore vertical distances when moving and can be placed atop climbable terrain without moving a vertical distance.

Falling

If a model without **Flight** or **Float** is moved off an elevation by a game effect or elects to fall down from an elevation, place the model at the base of the elevation. A model falling at least 3" suffers a Damage Flip of 2/4/6 for each full 3" fallen. Total the Damage Flips and inflict that amount of damage on the model (Damage, p.44). These Damage Flips may not be Cheated. Models with bases overlapped by the falling model after it lands are Pushed away from the model's base in a direction of their controller's choosing until their bases are no longer covered by the fallen model.

Disengaging

During its activation, a model may wish to disengage from one or more enemy models by moving out of opposing models' melee ranges. A model can do so, but this disengagement may be blocked by an enemy combatant (Disengaging, p.48).

PLACEMENT EFFECTS

A *placement effect* changes an in-play model's location on the table without using a movement effect to travel through terrain or other models, or brings a model that is not currently in play onto the table. A model's base must be placed where it can fit, and may not be placed so that any portion of it is further than the placement effect permits.

Any time the model changes its location on the table or is brought into play by Place, Replace, or Switch, it is affected by a placement effect.

Place

Place is a placement effect which requires a model to be Placed in a specific location. If the model is being Placed in base contact with another model, there must be room for the model to fit.

When a model is Placed in a new location, effects limiting the distance it may move immediately end. Unless stated otherwise, a model's base must be placed completely within any stated range.

Replace

Some placement effects require a model (or models) to Replace one another. When a model(s) Replaces another, place that model in base contact with the model it is replacing, then remove the replaced model from play. There must be room for the model to fit. Any effects on the model(s) being replaced are applied to all Replacing models, including any **Wounds** suffered, which must be divided as evenly as possible between them.

The Replacing model(s) continues the activation using any general AP the replaced model(s) had remaining. If there are not enough general AP to evenly divide between the Replacing models, their controller divides them as evenly as possible and decides which model receives any remainder. The Replacing model(s) can use their specific AP during this activation if any of the replaced models had not already used the same talent or spell. When multiple models replace a single model, they complete their activations using the simultaneous activation rules.

Switch

The Switch placement effect requires multiple models to exchange locations. When Switching models, each model is relocated to the other model's position and must cover as much of the other model's base area as possible. When a model Switches locations, effects limiting the distance it may move immediately end.

COMBAT

Malifaux games will usually be decided by a Crew's skill with bullets, blades, or claws. Combat is resolved using opposed Duels.

General Combat Actions

(1) Strike: The model (attacker) targets another model or piece of breakable terrain (defender) within range and performs an opposed Duel using the **Combat (Cb)** value of one of its Weapons against the defender's **Defense (Df)** value, shown as **Cb → Df**. A model must have a melee Weapon to make a melee **Strike** or a ranged Weapon to make a ranged **Strike**.

(1) Defensive Stance: This must be the first Action the model takes during its activation. Until the End Closing Phase, this model's Defense Flips receives 🎴🎴 when defending in a melee or ranged attack Duel. The model also receives -2/-2 **Wk/Cg** until the End Closing Phase.

(2) Focus: The model performs a melee or ranged **Strike**. The **Strike's** Attack Flip and Damage Flip receive 🎴. Weapons that require more than 1 AP to make a Strike cannot be **Focused**.

MELEE BASICS

- All models have access to the melee weapon **Bash** with Rg ⚔ 1, **Cb 3**, and **Dg 0/1/2**, even though it is not listed on their stat cards.
- A model's melee range is the **Rg** of any of its ⚔ Weapons.
- A weapon with a range that includes the ⚔ icon is considered a melee Weapon.
- Models in range of an enemy's melee Weapon, or with an enemy model within their melee Weapon range, are said to be **engaged** in melee, or engaged. Models may check their melee range to confirm whether they are engaged with or engaging enemy models at any time.

1" Melee Range   2" Melee Range   2" Melee Range

ENGAGED DIAGRAM

Francisco and Som'er Teeth Jones are **engaged** because they are within each other's melee range.

Francisco and Gremlin 1 are engaged because Gremlin 1 is within Francisco's melee range, even though Gremlin 1 does not have Francisco in his melee range.

- A model making a **Strike** with a with a melee (⚔) Weapon is making a melee attack and any modifiers that affect models making melee attacks apply.

Elevated Terrain and Melee

Models wishing to attack targets on elevated terrain determine their distance to the target as follows:

Flat Elevations:
- Models attacking down a flat elevation add the difference between the target's **Ht** and the elevation's **Ht** to their distance to the target.
- Models attacking up a flat elevation add the difference between their **Ht** and the flat elevation's **Ht** to the distance to the target.

> *Example: A model with a melee weapon (**Rg** 2) on a **Ht** 2 flat elevation can only reach a **Ht** 2 target up to 2" away if the model was standing on the edge of the flat elevation. That same model could reach a **Ht** 1 model if it was within 1" of the elevation.*
>
> *A **Ht** 2 model standing at the bottom of that same flat elevation with **Rg** 2 weapon could reach up to 2" across the elevation if it was in base contact with the bottom. However, if it the flat elevation was **Ht** 3 and its intended target stood 2" back atop the elevation it would not be able to reach (elevation's **Ht** 3 – model's **Ht** 2 = +1 to the distance).*

Sloped Elevations:
- Models attacking up or down sloped elevations determine distance to their target as normal.

Melee Modifiers

Focus	Attacker's Attack and Damage Flips receive ⬛.
Charge	Attacker's Damage Flip receives ⬛.
Defensive Stance	Defender's Defense Flip receives ⬛ ⬛.
Paired Weapon	Attacker's Attack Flip receives ⬛.

RANGED BASICS

- A weapon with a range that includes the ⌐ icon is considered a ranged Weapon.
- Models engaged in melee cannot make ranged attacks.
- A model making a Strike with a ranged (⌐) Weapon is making a ranged attack and any modifiers that affect models making ranged attacks apply.
- Models without a ranged (⌐) Weapon cannot make ranged (⌐) **Strikes**.

Ranged Modifiers

Target in Soft Cover	Attacker's Attack Flip receives ⊟.
Target in Hard Cover	Attacker's Attack Flip receives ⊟. Target receives **Armor +1.**
Firing into Melee	Defender receives +1 **Df** for each enemy model it is engaged with.
Focus	Attacker's Attack and Damage Flips receive ⬛.
Defensive Stance	Defender's Defense Flip receives ⬛ ⬛.
Paired Weapon	Attacker's Attack Flip receives ⬛.

STRIKE SEQUENCE

Models making a ranged or melee **Strike** use the **Strike** attack sequence.

Strike Attack Sequence

1. Declare Target, then Check Range
2. Strike Duel
   a. Flip Starting Attack and Defense Totals
   b. Change Starting Totals or Pass
   c. Determine Final Duel Totals
   d. Declare Triggers
   e. Determine Success
   f. Apply Duel Results

STRIKE ATTACK SEQUENCE – DETAILS

1. Declare Target, then Check Range

A model must be within the attacker's LoS to be declared the target of a **Strike**. If there are no targets within the attacker's LoS, the **Strike** fails. A model cannot target itself with a **Strike**.

Once a target in LoS has been declared the target of the **Strike**, ensure that the target is in range by measuring the distance between the two models. All range measurements in Malifaux are made from the attacking model's base edge to the closest point on the target model's base edge. If the distance is shorter than or equal to the attack's **Rg**, the target is in range; proceed to **2. Strike Duel** below. Otherwise, the target is out of range, is not a legal target, and the **Strike** fails.

2. Strike Duel

Perform the **Strike (Cb → Df)** Duel. Some **Strikes** may use other stats for the attacker and/or defender and are indicated in their descriptions.

A. Flip for Starting Attack and Defense Totals. The attacker and defender each flip one Fate Card (**Attack Flip** and **Defense Flip** respectively) + one Fate Card for each fate card modifier (🟦 or 🖃) applied to their respective flips. If the flip had a positive modifier (one or more 🟦), then the model chooses which of the flipped Cards to keep. If the flip had a negative modifier (one or more 🖃), then the model must choose the lowest value Card. If one of the flipped Cards was the Red Joker, the model may choose to keep it regardless of fate modifier. If one of the flipped Cards was the Black Joker, the player **must** keep it regardless of any other Card flipped, including the Red Joker. Place the chosen Card on top of any other flipped Cards.

Starting Duel total = Fate Card value and suit + stat value and suit + applicable modifiers

Compare the models' starting totals.

- The model with the higher total is winning the Duel. If the totals are tied, the attacker is winning the Duel.

B. Change Starting Totals or Pass. Starting with the losing model, each model may use either or both options below, in the order listed, but can use each option only once. A model may choose to pass and not use either option. If both models pass changing their totals, move on to Step C below.

- **Cheat Fate:** The losing model may replace the flipped Fate Card with a Control Card from its Control Hand. Place the Control Card on top of any other Cards the model has in play. **A model cannot Cheat Fate if it has a negative fate modifier or its current Fate Card is the Black Joker.**
- **Use Soulstones:** If the model has the Use Soulstones ability, it may discard a Soulstone to flip a second Fate Card and add its value and suit to the Duel total. Place this card next to the Fate Card in play. If the Black Joker is flipped, it adds nothing to the total; it does not replace the original card. **A model can Use Soulstones even if it has a negative fate modifier or its current Fate Card is the Black Joker.**

C. Determine Final Duel Totals. This is determined after both models have had an opportunity to change their starting Duel totals.

Final Duel totals = Fate Card value and suit (original or replacement from Cheating Fate) + stat value and any suits + applicable modifiers + value and suit of any Fate Card from Using Soulstones

D. Declare Triggers. Starting with the model with the lower total or the defender if the totals are tied, each model may now declare one Trigger that it has met the suit requirements for. The Trigger's description will indicate when its effects are applied.

E. Determine Success. The difference between the attacker's and defender's totals is called the *combat total*.

- If the attacker's final Duel total is equal to or greater than the defending model's final Duel total, it wins the Duel and hits the defender. **(Success)**
- Otherwise, the defender wins the Duel and is not hit by the attack. **(Failure)**

F. Apply Duel Results. Any additional effects as a result of the Duel, such as Triggers, are applied as indicated in their descriptions.

If the attacker hit the defender with the attack, the attacker inflicts damage (see Damage below) as modified on the combat total modifier chart.

Combat Total Modifier Chart

If the combat total was...	0	1-5	6-10	11+

FIRING INTO MELEE

Models may make ranged **Strikes** and cast ranged (☞) attack Spells into melee combat. Because the combatants in a melee are not standing still during the fight, the attacking model may wind up hitting another target than the one it intended to. It could even hit an ally with this ranged attack.

The attacker declares the target of the ranged attack, and then flips one Fate Card for the target and each model in the target's melee range as well as any enemy model engaged with the target, regardless of LoS to those models. Flip two Fate Card for models with a **Ht** of 3 or more. The model with the lowest value card becomes the new target of the attack. In the case of models tied for the lowest card, the attacking model may choose its target from those tied models.

Resolve the ranged attack as normal. The target receives +1 **Df** (or +1 to its Resist stat if resisting a ranged (☞) attack Spell) for each enemy model it is engaged with. If the attacker wins the Duel, the target is hit as normal. If the attacking model loses the Duel, the attack is a miss.

DAMAGE

Models may suffer **Damage (Dg)** or **Wounds (Wd)** during an Encounter.

Incoming **Damage**, including any increases or reductions from Triggers or effects, is totaled, and then inflicted as **Wounds** on the recipient. A model can use a Talent or cast a Spell that inflicts **Dg** on itself as long as it is not targeting itself with an attack Spell.

Models may also suffer **Wounds** directly. Incoming **Wd**, including any increases or reductions from Triggers or effects, are totaled, and then inflicted on the recipient. Effects which increase or reduce **Dg** do not affect **Wd** inflicted directly, and vice versa. A model cannot use a Talent or cast a Spell that requires it to inflict **Wd** on itself if it would reduce its own **Wounds** to 0.

When a model suffers **Wd**, reduce its remaining **Wd** stat by one point for each point of **Wd** suffered. Models can only suffer as many **Wounds** as they have remaining, and can never be reduced to negative **Wounds**. A model reduced to 0 **Wd** will be removed from the game as killed unless an effect that could prevent the **Wd** or heal the model to 1 or more **Wd** is applied.

> *Examples: A Punk Zombie must inflict up to 3 **Wd** on itself when casting the **Self-Mutilate** Spell. If the Punk Zombie has 3 or fewer **Wd** remaining, it could not inflict the full 3 **Wd** on itself when casting the spell as this would reduce its **Wd** to 0.*

> *Papa Loco's **Take Ya With Me** inflicts 6 **Dg** on Papa. Because it inflicts **Dg** and not **Wd**, Papa could use it regardless of the number of **Wd** he had remaining.*

The Damage Flip

For most attacks, **Damage** is listed as three numbers separated by slashes.

> *Example: Sonnia Criids's Runed Blade **Damage (Dg)** is 2/3/5.*

These numbers represent the severity of the damage (from left to right) as **Weak**, **Moderate**, or **Severe**. When making a **Damage Flip**, flip a Fate Card and compare its value (not the suit) to the Damage Chart below to determine the amount of damage the hit inflicted.

Perdita Ortega is firing into melee. She wants to target Gremlin 1. Because other models are involved in the melee, she must flip cards to determine whom the Strike targets. The Warpig and Niño are within Gremlin 1's melee range, while Gremlin 1 is within Francisco's melee range. She flips a card for everyone involved; flipping a 4 for Gremlin 1, a 4 for Francisco, a 5 and 7 for the Warpig, and an 8 for Niño. Because neither Gremlin 1 nor Gremlin 2 is in each others 1" melee range, Gremlin 2 is not a potential target. Perdita's lowest two cards are tied between Francisco and Gremlin 1, allowing her to choose Gremlin 1 as her target.

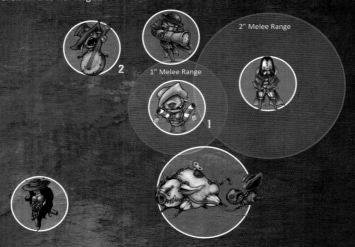

2" Melee Range

1" Melee Range

Combat

A model may Cheat Fate on a Damage Flip unless one or more ⊟ apply to the flip. Triggers declared during a Duel, or damage modifiers from game effects, are applied after a model has decided whether or not to Cheat Fate.

Jokers

When a Black Joker is flipped for damage, or played while Cheating Fate, the attacker must use it. If the Black Joker was flipped for damage, the model flipping it cannot Cheat Fate and the Damage Flip inflicts no damage.

When a Red Joker is flipped for damage, or played while Cheating Fate, it inflicts Severe damage plus a second Damage Flip's worth of damage. The combined total plus any additional damage modifiers is then inflicted. If the Red Joker is flipped as part of a Damage Flip with one or more ⊟, the Red Joker can be selected instead of the lowest value Card. If the Card flipped after the Red Joker is the Black Joker, it adds no additional damage, but does not negate the Severe damage amount.

Damage Chart

If the value of the flip is...	Black Joker	1-5	6-10	11+	Red Joker
The damage is...	No Damage	Weak	Moderate	Severe	Severe + another Damage Flip

Damage Flip Example: *A Terror Tot's Claw **Dg** is 1/3/4 and flips for damage with no fate modifiers. The flipped Fate Card is a 4 (inflicting Weak damage, 1 point). The Terror Tot decides that isn't enough and Cheats Fate, replacing the 4 with an 11 from its Hand (inflicting Severe damage, 4 points).*

The same Terror Tot flips for damage later, but with a ⊟ to the Damage Flip. It flips a 4 and the Red Joker. Normally, it would have to use the 4 as that was the lowest card in the flip, but it can instead use the Red Joker. It then flips an 8 for its second card. The total inflicted from its attack would be 7 points, 4 for the Red Joker's Severe plus 3 more for the additional Moderate flip.

BLASTS

When a Damage stat includes one or more 🗯, whether any 🗯 are generated depends on the Damage Flip. Flip for damage as normal. If the flipped severity indicates one or more 🗯, Place the first 🗯 covering a portion of the target model's base. Each additional 🗯 must be placed so that it is touching but not overlapping another 🗯.

Any model, other than the initial target, touched by one or more 🗯 suffers damage one severity lower than what was inflicted on the target. Any additional effects suffered by the target, such as the effects of Triggers, are not suffered by the other models touched by the 🗯 unless specifically stated otherwise.

If a Red Joker is flipped for damage, the defender suffers the total damage, but additional 🗯 are only generated off the Severe damage amount. Do not add 🗯 based on the additional damage Card flipped. Models touched by any 🗯 generated by a Red Joker suffer Moderate damage.

Blast Placement Diagram #1

Gremlin 1 is struck by a weapon which causes damage with multiple blasts (☁☁☁). ☁#1 must be placed touching Gremlin 1, since it was the target of the attack. Each additional ☁ must be placed to touch a previously placed ☁. In this example, ☁#2 is placed to damage Gremlin 2 (while touching ☁#1), and ☁#3 is placed to damage Gremlin 3.

Blast Placement Diagram #2

This diagram shows Gremlin 1 being struck by a weapon which causes a ☁. The ☁ may be placed to include Gremlin 2 on the other side of the **Ht** 2 wall, since the ☁ is **Ht** 3, it has LoS over the wall.

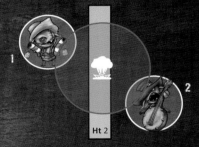

Ht 2

Blast Placement Diagram #3

This diagram shows Gremlin 1 struck by a weapon which causes ☁☁☁. The ☁☁☁ can be placed to 'snake around' a blocking wall with a **Ht** too tall for the ☁ to have LoS over.

Blast Placement Diagram #4

This diagram shows Gremlin 1 struck by a weapon which causes a ☁. Gremlin 2 can be caught in the ☁ regardless of the height of the blocking area.

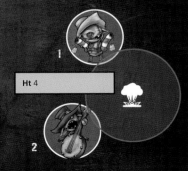

HEALING

Game effects that *heal* **Wounds** cannot raise a model's **Wound** total higher than its printed **Wounds** stat. Any **Wounds** healed over the printed stat value are lost. When an Ability or event calls for a Healing Flip, flip one Fate Card. This flip cannot be Cheated or added to by Soulstones. Compare the flipped card's value to the Healing Chart below to determine the number of **Wounds** the model is able to heal. When a model flips the Red Joker during a Healing Flip, it heals all **Wounds** previously suffered.

Healing Chart

If the value of the flip is...	Black Joker	1-5	6-10	11+	Red Joker
The # of **Wd** healed is...	Nothing	1	2	3	Heal all **Wd**

PREVENTING WOUNDS

A model with the **Use Soulstones** Ability can discard one Soulstone to prevent **Wd** it is about to suffer. Before the model suffers **Wd,** it discards a Soulstone and then flips one Fate Card (*Prevention Flip*), referring to the Wound Prevention Chart for the results. Reduce the number of **Wd** the model suffers by the amount listed in the chart. If the model flips the Red Joker, all **Wounds** it would have suffered are prevented. If the flip prevents more **Wd** than were incoming, the additional prevented **Wd** are lost; the model does not heal **Wd** previously suffered.

Wound Prevention Chart

If the value of the flip is...	Black Joker	1-5	6-10	11+	Red Joker
The # of **Wd** prevented is...	Nothing	1	2	3	All Incoming **Wd**

DISENGAGING

Models cannot simply move past enemy models without risking an attack. To represent this, the moment a moving enemy model would leave a model's longest melee range, that model may interrupt the enemy's move and attempt to *block* it by making one melee **Strike**, called a *disengaging Strike*, targeting that enemy model. No Triggers can be declared by the blocking or moving model during this **Strike**. The **Strike** does not inflict **Dg** or **Wd** on the moving model if it hits. Instead, if the **Strike** is a hit, the Action of the disengaging model ends immediately. Models being Pushed, Placed, or Switched cannot be blocked when they leave an enemy model's melee range.

Combat Example:

*Lady Justice **Charges** Madame Sybelle, intending to put the foul abomination back in the grave where she belongs.*

A. Models Flip for Starting Attack and Defense Totals. *Lady Justice (**Cb** 7♠) flips a 3▦, making her starting attack total 10♠▦. Madame Sybelle (**Df** 5) flips a 8♥, making her starting defense total 13♥.*

B. Models Change Starting Duel Totals or Pass. *Because Lady Justice is currently losing the Duel, she has to change her total or pass. She Cheats, replacing her 3▦ with a 9♠ from her Control Hand. She also wants to make sure she inflicts as much damage as possible on Madame Sybelle, so she discards one Soulstone from her Crew's Soulstone Pool, adding the flip (9♥).*

Although Madame Sybelle cannot raise her total high enough for Lady Justice to miss, she can reduce the difference in their totals enough that she may be able to survive the attack. She replaces her 8♥ with a 13▦ from her Control Hand.

C. Models Determine Final Duel Totals. *Lady Justice's attack total is now 25♠♠♥ (7♠+9♠+9♥). Madame Sybelle's defense total is now 18▦ (5+13▦).*

D. Models Declare Triggers. *Madame Sybelle does not have any Triggers which use her **Df** stat, so she passes on declaring a Trigger. Lady Justice, on the other hand, has two **Cb** Triggers she could declare: **Critical Strike** and **Final Repose**. She elects to declare the **Critical Strike** Trigger, which will add +1 **Dg** to her damage total for each ♠ in her Duel total. In this case, +2 **Dg** (♠♠ in her Duel total).*

E. Determine Success. *Lady Justice's 25 is higher than Madame Sybelle's 18, so Lady Justice has hit Madame Sybelle with her Greatsword. Lady Justice's combat total is the difference between their totals – in this case, 7.*

F. Apply Duel Results. *Lady Justice now makes her Damage Flip. Because Madame Sybelle reduced the combat total below 11+, there is no combat total modifier (combat total 7 = no modifier).*

*Totaling up any other Damage Flip modifiers, we see that Lady Justice **Charged** (▲), her Greatsword inflicts ▲ on Damage Flips, and Madame Sybelle's **Hard to Wound 1** Ability modifies Damage Flips by ⊟, making Lady Justice's flip modifier a ▲ (▲+▲+⊟).*

*Lady Justice flips two Cards, a 1♥ and a 6▦, and chooses to keep the 6▦. Because her fate modifier was ▲, she can Cheat Fate on the Damage Flip and elects to, replacing the 6▦ with the Red Joker from her hand. She flips a second Card (10♠). Looking at her Greatsword's **Dg** stat, she will be inflicting 12 **Dg** on Madame Sybelle (6 points for the Greatsword's Severe + 4 points for its Moderate + 2 points from Critical Strike), laying Madame Sybelle low in one swing.*

*But before Madame Sybelle is removed from the game, she is able to take one last Action thanks to her **Slow to Die** Ability. Lady Justice steels herself for the desperate blow...*

MAGIC

General Magic Actions

(#) Cast: This model spends the AP listed before the Spell's name and casts the Spell. Casting a **(0)** Spell counts as a model's **(0)** Action for its activation.

(2) Channel: This model **Casts** a **(1)** Spell. The casting receives ⊞ to both its Casting and any Damage Flips.

(1) Drain Souls: Leaders Only. Sacrifice up to three friendly models within 6", ignoring LoS. The Crew's Soulstone Pool gains one Soulstone for each model sacrificed. Each time a leader takes the **Drain Souls** Action, every non-leader model in the Crew receives a cumulative -1 **Wp** for the remainder of the Encounter. Models with the Insignificant Characteristic cannot be sacrificed by Drain Souls.

Spell Basics

- Spells require LoS to their targets unless otherwise indicated in their description. Spells affecting more than one target do not affect targets outside the caster's LoS. Spells that generate an aura (◐) or pulse ((ẋ)) area effect, or affect all models within a certain range, do not require a target to cast.
- A model casting a Spell with a ⫻ or ☞ icon in its **Rg**, or one that requires a Resist Duel, is casting an attack Spell.
- Spells with a ⫻ or ☞ icon in their **Rg** are melee and ranged attack Spells respectively and follow the targeting rules for those types of attacks. Modifiers that affect melee or ranged attacks affect these Spells as well.

Spell Details

Spells are listed in the rules as follows:

(#) Spell Name (CC: # / Rst: # / Rg: #)
Spell Description.

Spell Name: The name of the spell, duh.

(CC) Casting Cost: A spell's Casting Cost is the TN the caster needs to equal or exceed to successfully cast the Spell with a simple **Ca → CC** Duel.

> *Casting Cost Example: Shriek has a Casting Cost of 14✗. Madame Sybelle's simple Duel total must be at least 14 and contain at least one ✗ for it to be successful. She has a **Ca** 6✗, so she has already met the suit requirement to cast the spell, meaning that it doesn't need to be present on the Fate Cards, and only needs a Fate Card of 8 or higher to successfully cast the spell.*

(Rst) Resist Duel Required: If a Rst stat is listed for a Spell, when it is successfully cast any model that could be affected by it must win a Resist Duel **(Stat → Final Casting Total) by exceeding the casting total** or suffer the spell's effects. The Resist Duel occurs after the caster has completed its Casting Duel and successfully cast the Spell. Friendly models that could be affected by Spells requiring Resist Duels must resist as normal, but when determining final totals, can choose to tie the casting total and suffer the Spell's effects.

(Rg) Spell Range: A Spell's **Rg** is the furthest effective distance, in inches, the Spell can reach. Spells that target the caster have a range of **C**. Spells with ❶ or (ϟ) in their ranges follow the rules for Aura and Pulse effects respectively (p.20). Spells with a ∥ or ⌒ icon in their **Rg** are melee and ranged attack Spells respectively and follow the targeting rules for those types of attacks. Modifiers that affect melee or ranged attacks affect these Spells as well.

Spell Description: Describes the Spell's effects. This may include any additional casting restrictions such as special targeting rules, or additional requirements for casting the Spell. When a Spell lists *additional casting requirements* in the first line of its description, these requirements must be met during the Casting Duel or the Spell will fail. These requirements include: the caster suffering **Wd**, sacrificing/discarding Counters or Soulstones, sacrificing/killing friendly models (or the casting model), or others indicated as *"AR: requirement."*

CASTING SPELLS

A model must win a simple **Ca → Casting Cost** Casting Duel to cast a spell. If the spell does not require a Resist Duel, apply the Spell's effects when a model wins the Casting Duel. If the spell requires a Resist Duel, after the acting model wins the Casting Duel, any models who would be affected must perform a Resist Duel against the casting total to resist its effects. The Spell's effects are only applied if the Resist duel is unsuccessful.

Magic

Casting Sequence

1. Declare Spell and Target
2. Casting Duel
   a. Caster Flips Starting Casting Total
   b. Caster Changes Starting Total or Passes
   c. Caster Determines Final Duel Total
   d. Caster Declares a Trigger
   e. Caster Determines Success
3. Resist Duels (if necessary)
   a. Resisting Model Flips Starting Resist Total
   b. Resisting Model Changes Starting Total or Passes
   c. Resisting Model Determines Final Duel Total
   d. Caster Meets Additional Requirements
   e. Resisting Model Declares a Trigger
   f. Resisting Model Determines Success
4. Apply Spell Effects

1. Declare Spell and Target

The model declares the Spell it is casting, spends the required AP and meets any other requirements (such as discarding cards or suffering **Dg** or **Wd**), and nominates a target within LoS if one is required. Measure range to the target from the caster's base edge to the closest base edge of the target. If the target is not in the Spell's range, and/or if the caster cannot meet the Spell's additional requirements (if any), the Action fails.

2. Casting Duel

Once the target has been determined to be within range and LoS, perform a simple **Ca → CC** Casting Duel.

A. Caster Flips for Starting Duel Total. The caster flips one Fate Card (*Casting Flip*) + one Fate Card per fate modifier (🔷 or ▭). If the flip had a positive modifier (one or more 🔷), then the caster chooses which of the flipped Cards to keep. If the flip had a negative modifier (one or more ▭), then the caster must choose the lowest value Card. If one of the flipped Cards was the Red Joker, the player may choose to keep it regardless of fate modifier. If one of the flipped Cards was the Black Joker, the player **must** keep it regardless of any other Card flipped, including the Red Joker. Place the chosen Card on top of any other flipped Cards.

Caster's Starting Casting Duel total = Fate Card's value and suit + Ca value and any suits + applicable modifiers

- If the starting Duel total is equal to or greater than the Spell's Casting Cost and includes at least one of each suit in the CC, the caster is winning the Duel. (**Success**)
- If the starting total is less than the Spell's Casting Cost and/or is missing one or more of the required suits, the caster is losing the Duel. (**Failure**)

Casting Modifiers

Channel	Caster's Casting and Damage Flips receive 🔷.

B. Caster Changes Starting Total or Passes.
The caster may use either or both options below, in the order listed, but can use each option only once. A model may choose not to use either option and instead move on to Step C.

- **Cheat Fate:** The caster may replace the flipped Fate Card with a Control Card from its Control Hand. Place the Control Card on top of any other Cards the model has in play. **A model cannot Cheat Fate if it has a negative fate modifier or its current Fate Card is the Black Joker.**
- **Use Soulstones:** If the caster has the **Use Soulstones** Ability, it may discard a Soulstone to flip a second Fate Card and add its value and suit to the Duel total. Place this card next to the Fate Card in play. If the Black Joker is flipped, it adds nothing to the total; it does not replace it. **A model can Use Soulstones even if it has a negative fate modifier or its current Fate Card is the Black Joker.**

C. Caster Determines Final Duel Total. This is determined after the caster has had an opportunity to change its starting Duel total.

Final Duel total = Fate Card value and suit (original or replacement from Cheating Fate) + stat value and any suits + applicable modifiers + value and suit of any Fate Card from Using Soulstones

D. Caster Meets Additional Requirements

If there are any additional requirements that must be met in order for the Spell to be cast, they must be met now or the spell immediately fails. These requirements are found in the first sentence of the Spell's description and include: the caster suffering **Wd**, sacrificing/discarding Counters or Soulstones, sacrificing/killing friendly models (or the casting model), or other requirements indicated as "*AR: [requirement]*."

E. Caster Declares a Trigger. The caster may now declare that it is using one Trigger that it has met the suit requirements for. The Trigger's description will indicate when its effects are applied.

F. Caster Determines Success.

- If the caster's final Duel total (the **casting total**) is equal to or greater than the CC, includes at least one of each suit in the TN, and the caster has met any additional requirements for the Spell, the caster has won the Duel and has successfully cast the Spell. (**Success**)
- Otherwise, the caster has lost the Duel and the Spell is not cast. If the Spell can be cast a limited number of times, this attempt does not count toward that limit. (**Failure**)

> *Casting Example: Ramos (Ca 8▩) casts **Electrical Fire** (CC: 14▩/Rst: Df / Rg ⌐12) at a target in LoS. After determining that the target is in range, Ramos makes his Casting Flip. His flip is a 4✕, making his starting casting total 12▩✕. He uses a Soulstone to increase his total, flipping and adding an 8▩, making his final casting total 20▩✕▩, which satisfies the casting cost for **Electrical Fire**. The spell is cast successfully. He declares he is using his **Surge Ca**(▩▩▩) Trigger. Since **Electrical Fire** requires a Resist Duel, the target must now resist the spell before Ramos makes his Damage Flip.*

3. Resist Duels

A model must perform a simple **Resist Duel (stat → caster's casting total)** if it is affected by a successfully cast Spell with a **Rst** stat indicated. Resist Duels use only the casting total's value as a TN; suits in the casting total are ignored.

When a spell could affect multiple models, all potentially affected models perform Resist Duels in an order of their controller's choosing. When more than one controller has models affected, use the turn's activation order (p.31) to determine which controller performs his or her models' Duels first.

A. Resisting Model Flips for Starting Duel Total. The resisting model flips one Fate Card (Resist Flip) + one Fate Card per fate modifier (⊕ or ⊖). If the flip had a positive modifier (one or more ⊕), then the resisting model chooses which of the flipped Cards to keep. If the flip had a negative modifier (one or more ⊖), then the resisting model must choose the lowest value Card. If one of the flipped Cards was the Red Joker, the player may choose to keep it regardless of fate modifier. If one of the flipped Cards was the Black Joker, the player **must** keep it regardless of any other Card flipped, including the Red Joker. Place the chosen Card on top of any other flipped Cards.

Resisting model's Starting Casting Duel total = Fate Card's value and suit + Ca value and any suits + applicable modifiers

- If the starting Duel total is greater than the Spell's casting total, the resisting model is winning the Duel. (**Success**)
- If the starting total is equal to or less than the Spell's casting total, the model is losing the Duel. (**Failure**)

B. Resisting Model Changes Starting Total or Passes. The resisting model may use either or both options below, in the order listed, but can use each option only once. A model may choose to not use either option and instead move on to Step C.

- **Cheat Fate:** The resisting model may replace the flipped Fate Card with a Control Card from its Control Hand. Place the Control Card on top of any other Cards the model has in play. **A model cannot Cheat Fate if it has a negative fate modifier or its current Fate Card is the Black Joker.**
- **Use Soulstones**: If the resisting model has the **Use Soulstones** Ability, it may discard a Soulstone to flip a second Fate Card and add its value and suit to the Duel total. Place this card next to the Fate Card in play. If the Black Joker is flipped, it adds nothing to the total; it does not replace it. **A model can Use Soulstones even if it has a negative fate modifier or its current Fate Card is the Black Joker.**

C. Resisting Model Determines Final Duel Total. This is determined after the resisting model has had an opportunity to change its starting Duel total.

Final Duel total = Fate Card value and suit (original or replacement from Cheating Fate) + stat value and any suits + applicable modifiers + value and suit of any Fate Card from Using Soulstones

D. Resisting Model Declares a Trigger. The resisting model may now declare that it is using one Trigger that it has met the suit requirements for. The Trigger's description will indicate when its effects are applied.

E. Resisting Model Determines Success.
- If the resisting model's final Duel total is <u>**greater than the casting total**</u>, the resisting model has won the Duel and successfully resisted the Spell, avoiding its effects. This is slightly different than other simple Duels. Because the caster has already successfully cast the Spell, the resisting model's total must be higher than the casting total to successfully resist. (**Success**)
- If the resisting model's final Duel total is <u>**less than or equal to the casting total**</u>, the resisting model has lost the Duel and suffers the effects of the Spell. The difference between the casting total and the resist total counts as the combat total for any effects (such as Damage Flips) which require a combat total. (**Failure**)

4. Apply Spell Effects.
If the spell was cast successfully, apply the Spell's effects as indicated in its description.

Regardless of whether the spell was cast successfully and/or resisted, any additional effects, such as Triggers, are applied as indicated in their descriptions.

> *Resist Example: In the casting example above, Ramos successfully cast **Electrical Fire** against his target. Since Ramos' casting total was 20, the target must win a simple Df → 20 Resist Duel or suffer the spell's effects. The target's flip plus **Df** equals 13 after Cheating, which is lower than the 20 it needed to exceed. Ramos makes a Damage Flip using the difference between his casting and the target's resist totals as the combat total – in this case, 7 – so no fate modifiers apply to the Damage Flip.*

Summoned Models

Some game effects allow a model to be **Summoned** into the game. A Summoned model's base must be placed completely within 6" of the summoning model when it enters play. A model Summoned into base contact with another model must be placed in base contact with that model. A model cannot be Summoned if its base does not fit where it must be placed.

A Summoned model may activate during the turn it was summoned, but receives **Slow** (see p.34).

Models cannot Summon models, whether through Talents or Spells, while controlled by an enemy Crew.

Transform

Game effects may allow a model to **transform** into another model. When a model transforms, Replace the original model on the table with the new model. If there is not enough room for the new model, slide other models back until there is room. If the model still will not fit, the transformation fails. For voluntary transformations, the controller must have the correct model available to represent what is being transformed into. When forcing another player's model to transform, you must have the appropriate model available to represent its new form (unless that player has an appropriate model he or she would prefer to use).

The transformed model now uses the new model's statistic card but cannot use the new model's spells. Instead, the transformed model retains the spells of the original model. It is best to keep both models' cards next to each other to remind you what the model was before its transformation. The effect's description will indicate how the model's transformation ends, usually by taking a **(0)** Action if the transformation was voluntary. When the transformation ends, replace the new model with the original. Wounds suffered by and effects on the new form carry over to the original model.

A Crew member's strength of will often plays as important a role in a fight as their skill with a sword or pistol. In Malifaux, that strength of will can be challenged in a number of ways; some mundane, others supernatural in origin. These challenges are represented by the following morale rules.

Some game effects may influence whether a model falls back from the fight or battles on. These effects require the model to win a ***Morale Duel*** or fall back. Morale Duels are:
- A simple **Wp → TN** Duel which states in its description that it is a Morale Duel, or
- A Spell with a **Wp** Resist which states in its description that it is or counts as a Morale Duel.

In both of these instances, the model's starting flip is called the Morale Flip (in addition to it being a Resist Flip in the case of Spells).

A model which loses a Morale Duel is falling back (see below) in addition to any other effects it may suffer from losing the Morale Duel.

> ***Example:*** *The Special Location Event "Alone in the Dark" states that models losing Morale Duels are killed instead of falling back.*

Remember: Even though a Morale Duel usually uses the Wp stat, Wp Duels are not always Morale Duels. For example, many Spells and Weapons target Wp without being Morale Duels.

TERRIFYING →

Terrifying forces living models without the **Terrifying** Ability to make a Morale Duel when they:
- Begin their activation in a **Terrifying** effect's range.
- End an Action in a **Terrifying** effect's range.
- Enter a **Terrifying** effect's range and do not have either the Flight or Float Ability.
- Declare a Charge targeting a model with the **Terrifying** Ability.

The range of a model's Terrifying Ability is that Terrifying model's longest melee range.

If the model wins the Morale Duel, it ignores that **Terrifying** effect for as long as it remains in that effect's **Terrifying** range and the effect exists. If a **Terrifying** effect ends and later resumes, models within the range of the resumed effect will have to perform Morale Duels again.

> *Terrifying Example: The "Kid's Got a Knife!" Spell gives its caster the **Terrifying** Ability. At the end of each turn, the Spell ends. Models still in the caster's melee range that won the Morale Duel during the current turn will have to resolve another Morale Duel next turn if the Spell is cast again while they are in the caster's melee range.*

FALLING BACK

A model that loses a Morale Duel or is affected by an effect that forces a model to fall back is *falling back*. It must immediately make a fall back move. Until the falling back model rallies (see below), its starting flips for all Duels other than Morale Duels receive ⊟.

Fall Back Move

A model making a *fall back move* immediately moves double its **Wk** toward the closest table edge using the most direct route possible. This move is not considered to be an Action. During this fall back move, the model may choose to not intentionally move into an enemy model's melee range or into hazardous terrain if an alternate passable route exists. If the falling back model is engaged with the model that caused the lost Morale Duel, it falls back directly away from that model. Any disengaging movement by a falling back model can be blocked by enemy models. If the fall back move occurred during the model's activation, the activation immediately ends. **Paralyzed** models do not make fall back moves.

A model that cannot make a fall back move due to its position on the table does not move at all. If the model touches the table edge during the fall back move, it immediately stops. If the model was already touching the table edge when it was forced to make a fall back move, it is sacrificed instead. Any Counters carried by the model are removed from the game.

Rallying

A falling back model spends its next activation to *rally*. Until the end of that activation, the falling back model cannot perform any general or specific movement Actions and receives ⊟ to any Duels it must perform except for Morale Duels. After the end of the model's activation, it is no longer falling back, becomes *rallied,* and may continue to act as normal. Models passing their activation due to **Paralyzed** are rallied at the end of that activation.

TERRAIN AND TRAITS

Adding **terrain** to the playing area is one way to enhance game play. In addition to making the game more visually appealing, terrain provides several tactical options for Crews to exploit. Try covering at least half of the playing area with terrain, but any amount of terrain is acceptable as long as all players agree on the setup. Story and tournament Encounters may require the placement of specific types of terrain; simply follow the Encounter's instructions in these cases (Encounters, p.62).

When laying out the terrain, all players should agree on what effects each piece of terrain will have during the game. This will help to avoid situations later in the game where you and your opponent may disagree as to whether that patch of brush provided cover or not.

Terrain, just like models, has both a **Ht** and a base. There is no standard base size for terrain because of the wide variety of terrain options available. Whatever area of the table the terrain piece's footprint covers is considered its base. A terrain piece's **Ht** should be agreed upon before the game begins, or use the actual piece's height in inches as a quick **Ht** stat if needed.

Unless it has the impassable trait, terrain can be occupied by other items; these will typically be models. Terrain may only be targeted by game effects that specify thet they may target terrain.

TRAITS

Items in Malifaux possess one or more of the following **traits**.

Blocking
Terrain that blocks LoS. High walls and dense forests are examples of blocking terrain.
Effect: See p.15 for the blocking trait's effect on LoS and cover.

Breakable
Components that can be knocked down or destroyed during an Encounter. Breakable terrain has a Hardness value from 1 to 10. Doorways, windows, walls, and terrain that the players agree upon as being able to be destroyed during an Encounter are breakable. **Effect:** Breakable terrain is divided into sections, each with a Hardness value. Small breakable sections, such as a door, have a single Hardness. Longer sections, such as the walls of a shack, have a specified Hardness for each 3" of length. Models may target breakable terrain with attacks. The attack on breakable terrain hits automatically; no attack Duel is required. When damaging Breakable/Targetable terrain, make a Damage Flip only (it may still be Cheated). Do not add blasts or perform any triggers. If the flip exceeds the section's Hardness, the section is destroyed and counts as severe terrain with a **Ht** of 0. Suggested Hardness: glass = 1, wood = 3, brick = 6, stone = 8, metal = 10.

Climbable
Vertical surfaces that allow models to locate themselves at various height levels on the surface. Ladders, vines, and ruined buildings are examples of climbable terrain. **Effect:** Models may move up and down climbable terrain. This movement costs double the distance moved.

Elevated

Terrain components that have a greater height than the general play area and permit models to stand atop them. Players should declare elevated terrain as either sloped (such as hills, and other slightly rising elevations) or flat (such as plateaus, bridge tops, and rooftops). **Effect:** See p.16 for how elevated terrain affects LoS.

Hazardous

Terrain components that cause damage to models moving through them. Acid pools or buildings set afire are examples of hazardous terrain. **Effect:** Models entering hazardous terrain flip for damage using the terrain type's damage stat. Use **Dg** 2/4/7 for all burning terrain, such as buildings and forest fires. Use **Dg** 3/6/killed for lava flows, acid pools, and other intensely deadly components. Models falling into deep chasms do not flip; they are automatically sacrificed. A model cannot Cheat the Damage Flip for hazardous terrain. Flying or Floating models ignore hazards unless players agree otherwise before the game begins. Models killed by hazards do not leave Corpse or Scrap Counters because when you drop your keys in something nasty like lava, they are gone, man!

Impassable

Terrain that models cannot move through. Cliffsides, deep water, and high walls are examples of impassable terrain. **Effect:** Models cannot move into or through impassable terrain. Impassable terrain also has the blocking trait.

Obscuring

Terrain that reduces the effectiveness of a ranged attack. Building corners and low walls are examples of obscuring terrain. **Effect:** See p.15 for the obscuring trait's effect on LoS and cover.

Open

Open terrain gives no penalties to movement or ranged attacks. All terrain is considered open terrain unless otherwise agreed upon before the game begins. **Effect:** None. This is the default trait for areas of the table with no terrain.

Severe

An area that is generally difficult to move through and slows movement. Rubble, brambles, and mud are examples of severe terrain. **Effect:** Movement through severe terrain costs double the distance moved.

Structure

Structures are enclosed pieces of terrain, typically buildings of some sort. **Effect:** Structures have the elevated (and a **Ht**), impassable, and blocking traits. Structures also have one or more entrances and windows. Entrances do not have the impassable trait and are the only way a model can enter a structure through a movement effect. Models inside a structure move as if it was open terrain. Windows are impassable and blocking but have a **Ht** of 1. Structures may possess multiple levels and, if so, models inside the structure may move between levels as if the structure had the climbable trait. Entrances can require a **(1) Interact** to open or close doors if players wish.

Water

Water components that may affect a model moving through it, as indicated in the model's statistics. Rivers and ponds are examples of Water terrain. **Effect:** Severe (see above). Some models receive bonuses or penalties for being in water.

Terrain Examples

Here are a few basic samples of how traits can be combined for terrain.

Bridge – flat elevation, open

Bridges across terrain with the water characteristic are considered open terrain for movement. Models may climb onto a bridge from a piece of terrain with the water trait using the rules for vertical movement as normal. At least one bridge per player is recommended if water features are being used, and each bridge should be at least 50mm wide.

Cliff – sloped elevation (Ht 4), impassible

A cliff is a sloping hill, but with one face impassable.

Fences – blocking, Ht 1

Fences are terrain with the blocking trait.

Hill – elevated (Ht 4)

A model on a hill is elevated. A hill could also have the sloping trait

Hut – breakable (Hd 2), structure (one entrance, one window), Ht 5

The hut is a **Ht** 5 structure with one entrance and one window. Because it is poorly constructed, it also has the breakable trait.

Shallow River – water, Ht 0

Models moving through the river must spend 2" for each 1" moved. Some models may be affected by the water trait as well.

Tree – obscuring, Ht 6

Trees are individual pieces of terrain that obscure LoS.

Woods – obscuring, severe, Ht 6

The base of a woods terrain piece has the obscuring and severe traits. Models have difficulty moving across the base, but are obscured.

ENCOUNTERS

To set up a Malifaux Encounter between two Crews, follow the Encounter Setup sequence below. Tournament or Story Encounters may change or ignore some of these steps. The goal of an Encounter of Malifaux is to have fun; players should feel free to ignore any of these steps when necessary. For example, if you do not have any terrain in your collection that would serve as a Gremlin Village, you may want to skip the random location generation step and simply play with the terrain you have.

1. Choose Encounter Size

Players begin by agreeing on the size of their Encounter. The **Encounter size** sets several factors in the Encounter: maximum Control Hand size, number of leaders per Crew, maximum starting Soulstone Pool size, and so forth. Once players have agreed on the Encounter size, they choose how many Soulstones they each have for hiring their Crews.

Example: A short Encounter between two Crew boxed sets is a 25 to 30 Soulstone Scrap.

After deciding on an Encounter size and the number of Soulstones available to Crews, shuffle one Fate Deck and place it within easy reach of all players.

Encounter Size	Scrap	Brawl
Soulstone Range	1-55	30-80
Maximum Control Hand Size per Crew	6	7
Number of Leaders per Crew	1	1-2
Maximum Starting Soulstone Pool Size per Crew	8	10

2. Choose Factions

Once the Encounter size is determined, each player must choose a Faction. Players do not need to select which leader(s) within that Faction they intend to play or hire any Minions at this time. When a player is allowed to hire multiple leaders, each leader must belong to either the Faction chosen by that player or be able to work with the selected Faction or other leader(s) already hired by meeting each model's hiring restrictions.

3. Choose Encounter Location

From abandoned Ghost Towns and the inhospitable Badlands to the very streets of the City, Encounters in Malifaux can take place in any number of unique *locations*. Players may either agree to choose a location (based on the terrain they have available), or use the following method to randomly determine a location for the Encounter.

One randomly-determined player flips two Fate Cards. The value of the first flip determines whether this is an indoor or outdoor Encounter. The value of the second flip then tells the players what location the Encounter takes place in. Additional information about these locations can be found beginning on p.74, including suggested terrain and random events or locations that may appear in the location.

Encounter Location

Black Joker	Flipping Player Chooses Location
1-8	Outdoor Location
9-13	Indoor Location
Red Joker	Non-Flipping Player Chooses Location

Outdoor Encounter Location

Black Joker	Flipping Player Chooses Location
1	Hag's Territory
2	Gremlin Village
3	Bayou's Edge
4	Bogs
5	Downtown
6	Industrial Zone
7	Slums
8	Quarantine Zone
9	Ruins
10	Mine
11	Pioneer/Ghost Town
12	Badlands
13	Mountains
Red Joker	Non-Flipping Player Chooses Location

Indoor Encounter Location

Black Joker	Flipping Player Chooses Location
1	Theater
2	Sewers
3	Arcanist's Lab
4	Resurrectionist's Lab
5	Guild Library
6	Necropolis
7	Guild Holding Facility
8	Warehouse
9	Research Facility
10	Cave/Mine System
11	Ancient Ruins
12	Large Tavern
13	Collapsed City Block
Red Joker	Non-Flipping Player Chooses Location

Terrain Setup

Malifaux is a skirmish game where every model counts! You can't make it too easy for the enemy to draw a bead on you from halfway across the table, so be sure to stack the odds against him with smart placement of terrain.

Once the Encounter location is determined, lay out terrain. A minimum playing size of 3' by 3' (36" x 36") is required for an Encounter of Malifaux. Anything from the dining room table to a gaming board or mat will work well for players, as long as the playing surface falls into this size range.

It is recommended that each square foot of the battlefield have approximately two to four pieces of terrain measuring at least 3" X 3" each to create an engaging and entertaining Encounter. All players should agree on the placement and type of terrain used. Story and Tournament Encounters will specify terrain (and of what type) in their descriptions.

Special location terrain should be set up during terrain setup unless otherwise stated in the special terrain's description. Some Strategies and Schemes require additional items to be placed on the table as directed by their descriptions (under **Setup**). These items should be placed during the Deploy Crews step unless otherwise stated in their description. These items do not displace terrain already set up on the table unless placing them on the terrain would mean all models could not reach the items. If so, move the terrain to a location on the table agreeable to all players.

> *Example:* During terrain setup, a wall was placed in the center of the table. If a player received the Treasure Hunt Strategy, which instructs the player to place a Treasure Counter in the center of the table, the wall would have to be moved to a mutually-agreed upon location before placing the Treasure Counter.

4. Choose Deployment Type

Once the terrain has been set up, players can either choose which deployment type they would like to use or randomly determine one player who then flips a Fate Card and refers to the chart below.

The dimensions included in the diagrams below are intended for the suggested 3' X 3' table size.

Deployment Chart

Black Joker	Flipping Player Chooses from the Deployment Areas in the Deployment Chart
1-4	**Diagonal** Draw a line between two opposite table corners. Each Crew's Deployment Zone begins 12.5" from that line.
5-9	**Standard** Each Deployment Zone comprises a 6" deep section, running the entire length of the table, on opposite table edges.
10-13	**Corners** Deployment Areas are 12" x 12" squares in two opposite corners of the table.
Red Joker	Non-Flipping Player Chooses from the Deployment Areas in the Deployment Chart

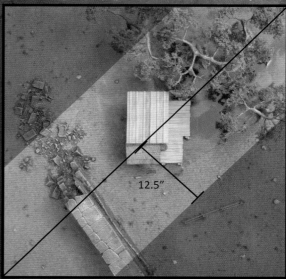

DIAGONAL DEPLOYMENT

12.5"

STANDARD DEPLOYMENT

CORNERS DEPLOYMENT

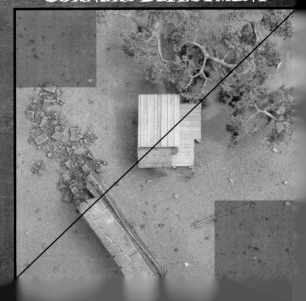

5. Determine Strategies

Now that the Encounter size, where it is located, and where the Crews will arrive have been determined, players now determine what their Crews are fighting over. Players agree on whether they are playing a **Core** or **Expanded** Encounter and then refer to the appropriate section below. Strategy descriptions and rules can be found in the Complete Strategies List starting on p.90.

All Strategies are public knowledge and should not be hidden from other players.

A **Strategy's** description includes its name, brief fiction, and some or all of the following:
  Any required objects such as terrain features, Counters, or Markers under **Setup**.
  Any required items such as terrain or Counters/Markers under **Setup**. These items are placed on the table before deploying Crews (p.73) or when indicated in their descriptions.
  What victory points (VP) are available for the player or players completing the Strategy under Victory. When a player scores a Strategy, they score all victory conditions that apply.
  All Markers are round 30mm bases, except when noted.

> *Example: <u>Victory</u>*
> *If at least three Dynamite Markers are armed at the end of the Encounter, you score **2 VP**.*
> *If all five Dynamite Markers are Armed at the end of the Encounter, you score **4 VP**.*
>
> *A Crew arming three or four Dynamite Markers in the A Line in the Sand Strategy would earn **2 VP**, but would earn **4 VP** if it managed to arm all five.*

Core Encounter

The Core Encounter Chart is designed for players who wish to play a more competitive Encounter. These Strategies represent the core causes of conflict in Malifaux, and players will find that each Faction has the tools available to accomplish them, as well as to stop their opponents from accomplishing their own Strategies. If a Core Encounter is chosen, players shuffle their Fate Decks and each flip a Fate Card to determine their Strategy for the Encounter. Details for these Strategies can be found starting on p.90. If both players flip the same Strategy, use the Shared version of that Strategy. Details for Shared Strategies can be found starting on p.95.

Core Encounter Chart	
okers	Player Chooses Strategy
-2	Treasure Hunt
-5	Destroy the Evidence
-8	Reconnoiter
-11	Claim Jump
2-13	Slaughter

Expanded Encounter

The Expanded Encounter Chart was designed to give players a nearly inexhaustible supply of Strategy interactions and provides unique challenges not found using the Core Encounter Chart. If an Expanded Encounter is chosen, randomly determine a player to shuffle his or her Deck and flip a Card. Refer to the Expanded Encounter Chart below to determine what type of Strategy players will be using in the Encounter.

Expanded Encounter Chart

Jokers	Flipping Player Chooses Type of Strategy (Individual, Shared, or Story)
1	Story Encounter OR Each Player Flips on the Individual Strategies Chart
2-8	Each Player Flips on the Individual Strategies Chart
9-12	One Player Flips on the Shared Strategy Chart
13	Story Encounter OR One Player Flips on the Shared Strategy Chart

(1-8) Individual Strategies Chart

Each player now shuffles his or her Fate Deck and flips a card. The Strategy a player flips applies to that player only. If all players flip or choose the same Strategy, play the Shared version of it instead. Details for these Strategies can be found starting on p.90. Details for the Shared versions of these Strategies can be found starting on p.95.

After all players have flipped, each player has one opportunity to re-flip the Strategy by reducing the number of Soulstones available for hiring models by one. Official Malifaux tournaments do not allow this Strategy re-flip.

Individual Strategies Chart

Black Joker	Opponent's Choice
1	A Line in the Sand
2	Claim Jump
3	Contain Power
4	Deliver a Message
5	Destroy the Evidence
6	Distract
7	Escape and Survive
8	Plant Evidence
9	Reconnoiter
10	Slaughter
11	Supply Wagon
12	Treasure Hunt
13	Turf War
Red Joker	Player's Choice

(9-13) Shared Strategy Chart

If the Expanded Encounter Chart directed the players to the Shared Strategy Chart, randomly determine one player to reshuffle his or her Deck and flip a Card. This Strategy applies to both players. Shared Strategy descriptions start on page 95.

Shared Strategy Chart

Black Joker	Opponent's Choice
1	Shared A Line in the Sand
2	Shared Claim Jump
3	Shared Contain Power
4	Shared Deliver a Message
5	Shared Destroy the Evidence
6	Shared Distract
7	Shared Escape and Survive
8	Shared Plant Evidence
9	Shared Reconnoiter
10	Shared Slaughter
11	Shared Supply Wagon
12	Shared Treasure Hunt
13	Shared Turf War
Red Joker	Player's Choice

Story Encounter Strategies

As with Shared Strategies, you only select one Strategy for all players, and multiple players may earn VP if they accomplish the required tasks. Players must decide if they are willing to include the option of playing the online catalog of Story Encounters, located at www.wyrd-games.net/storyencounters, before flipping on the Expanded Encounter Chart. If so, and a 1 or 13 is flipped, players should refer to the Story Encounters Chart found online. Otherwise, follow the instructions for the Encounter option. Story Strategies work much like Shared Strategies, except the setup and VP awards tend to be more involved and often include special rules. As Wyrd releases additional Story Encounters, we will provide expanded Story Encounter Strategy Charts.

6. Hire Crews

Once players have their Strategies set, they each decide on the best Crew to achieve their goals. Deduct a model's Soulstone Cost from the number of Soulstones available when it is hired. Players continue to hire models until the Soulstones run out or they choose to stop.

Remember, players who re-flipped for their Individual Strategies have one less Soulstone with which to hire models.

The following restrictions apply when hiring Crews:

General
- A Crew may only include models belonging to the player's chosen Faction, models with the Mercenary characteristic, and models permitted to join the Crew through any other special hiring rules. Models hired by a Crew must meet all special hiring rule restrictions or they cannot be hired.
- Models hired from outside the player's chosen Faction cost an additional Soulstone over their printed Soulstone Cost to hire.
- A maximum of the indicated number of a Rare model may be hired by a Crew in a Scrap. Twice that number may be hired by a Crew in a Brawl.
- A Crew cannot contain more than one copy of any Unique model it hires.
- Only one version of each named Unique model may be in a Crew. *Example: A Crew cannot hire both Hamelin and Hamelin the Plagued.*

Leaders
- In a Scrap, the player must choose one Master or a Henchman belonging to the chosen Faction as the Crew's leader.
- In a Brawl, the player must choose either one or two eligible Masters as the Crew's leaders. At least one of these Masters must belong to the player's chosen Faction, but both must be able to work with the Faction and/or other Master. If the player chooses only one Master to lead the Crew in a Brawl, he or she may increase their Soulstones available for hiring models by 10.

Masters
o Masters do not cost any Soulstones to hire.
o Masters add their Soulstone Cache to the Crew's starting Soulstone Pool (see below).

Henchmen
o When a Henchman leads a Crew in a Scrap, it costs 0 Soulstones to hire, just like a Master. Add the model's Henchman Resources bonus to the available Soulstones for hiring Minions. Henchmen cannot lead Brawl Crews.
o A Crew led by a Henchman has specific hiring restrictions as indicated under the Henchman's Special Forces Leader Ability.
o While leading a crew, a Henchman can be affected by anything that specifically affects Masters. Likewise, anything that cannot specifically affect a Master cannot affect a Henchman leading a Crew. A Henchman leading a Crew is considered a Master for Strategy and Scheme purposes.
o When a Crew is led by one or more Masters, it can hire one Henchman per Master, deducting the Henchman's Soulstone Cost from the Crew's available Soulstones. These Henchmen must belong to the same Special Forces group. When included in Master-led Crews, a Henchman's Henchman Resources bonus is ignored.
o A Henchman-led Crew's maximum starting Soulstone Pool is equal to its Henchman Resources bonus (see below).

Minions
- A Crew may only include Minions belonging to the player's chosen Faction unless a special rule allows them to be hired from other Factions.
- A player may hire as many Minions as the available Soulstones allow. Deduct the Soulstone Cost of each Minion hired from the Crew's available Soulstones.
- Minions with the Totem characteristic must be connected to a Master or Henchman in the Crew when hired. A Master/Henchman can be connected to one Totem at a time unless their description states otherwise. When a Master/Henchman is removed from the game, any Totems connected to it are immediately sacrificed.

Mercenaries
o A Crew may include up to two models with the Mercenary characteristic from any other Factions. Mercenaries from the player's chosen Faction do not count toward this total.

Special Forces
o A Crew may include up to two Faction or Mercenary models with the Special Forces [Group Name] characteristic per leader in their Crew. A Crew may only contain Special Forces models from one [Group Name]. If a Crew contains a Henchman who belongs to a Special Forces [Group Name], the two Special Forces model maximum is ignored for that group, but the limit of one Special Forces group in your Crew remains.

Starting Soulstone Pool
After players finish hiring Crews, any remaining unspent Soulstones form the player's starting *Soulstone Pool*. Crews led by one or more Masters add their Soulstone Caches to the Soulstone Pool. The maximum starting Soulstone Pool is 8 for Scraps and 10 for Brawls. Crews led by a Henchman do not add any additional Soulstones to the Pool. The maximum starting Soulstone Pool size in a Henchman-led Crew is equal to that Henchman's Henchman Resources bonus. In either case, Soulstones over the Crew's maximum Pool are lost. After the Encounter begins, there is no Soulstone Pool maximum.

> *Example:* After hiring, a Crew has two Soulstones left unspent. It is led by Lilith (Cache of 4). The Crew adds Lilith's four Soulstones to the two Soulstones remaining, creating a 6 Soulstone Pool. On the other hand, a Crew with two Soulstones left unspent led by the Henchman Collodi would have a starting Soulstone Pool of two.

All players must reveal the models hired for their Crew, as well as the starting size of their Soulstone Pool at this time.

Encounter Size	Maximum Starting Soulstone Pool Size
Scrap	8 (Master-led), Henchman Resource # (Henchman-led)
Brawl	10

7. Choose Schemes
Schemes are lesser objectives your Crew can attempt to achieve during the Encounter and should be kept secret from opponents. Players can select a number of Schemes based on the Encounter size. Players are not required to select Schemes if they do not want them. Scheme descriptions and rules can be found in the Master Schemes List starting on p.100.

A *Scheme's* description includes its name, brief fiction, and some or all of the following:
- Any limitations on who can choose the Scheme such as (Arcanists Only) or (Sonnia Criid Only).
- Any required items such as terrain features, Counters, or Markers under **Setup**.
- Any special rules that apply to the Scheme under **Special**. These items are placed on the table when indicated in the Scheme's description.
- What victory points (VP) are available for the player completing the Scheme and whether or not it can be announced before the Encounter begins under **Victory**. When scoring a Scheme, score all victory conditions that apply. A Scheme's **Announced** VP are only scored if the player completes the Scheme and it was announced after Crews are deployed (see 8. Deploy Crews on p.73).
- Players must state all details regarding the Scheme including any models or terrain nominated when it is announced (see below).

Encounter Size	Total # of Schemes
Scrap	0-2
Brawl	0-3

Players may choose to select fewer than the maximum number of Schemes for their Encounter size. Each Scheme not selected adds 2 Soulstones to the player's starting Soulstone Pool.

When the Encounter begins, daring players can choose to announce any of their eligible Schemes to their opponents. These Schemes are worth the additional VP listed if completed.

Some Schemes require a player to nominate a terrain feature or model. Terrain features and models can only be nominated by one Strategy and one Scheme per player at any time. That is, if a player chooses multiple Schemes which nominate enemy models, each Scheme must nominate a different enemy model.

There are three types of Schemes available to players: General Schemes, Faction Specific Schemes, and Master Specific Schemes. When choosing Schemes, any number of them may come from General Schemes. Players may choose one of their chosen Faction's Faction Specific Schemes per leader in their Crew. A player may choose one Master Specific Scheme per Master in their Crew.

8. Deploy Crews

Before deploying Crews, players should place any additional items on the table required by Strategies/Schemes/special location terrain rules. After players have hired their Crews and any additional terrain or Counters/Markers have been placed, players shuffle their Fate Decks and each flip a Card. If the flip is a tie, re-flip. The player with the highest Card nominates a player who chooses one of the shaded deployment areas. That player then deploys his or her entire Crew within the area. The other player deploys his or her Crew in the remaining deployment area.

Announced Schemes can be revealed once the Crews are deployed. Starting with the player who deployed his or her Crew first, each player may select and announce their Schemes. All details of an announced Scheme, including any requirements (nominated models, terrain, etc), must be announced at this time. These Schemes and the player's Strategy remain public knowledge throughout the Encounter.

After all Crews are deployed, all players re-shuffle their Fate Decks and start the Encounter!

Varying Encounter Length

A standard Malifaux Encounter lasts 6 turns but may carry on even longer. At the end of turn 6, the player who activated the last model in the turn flips a Fate Card. If the Card value is a 10 or higher, play another turn, but increase the value needed to continue the Encounter on next turn's flip by one. The Encounter ends when the flip is less than the value needed. *Example: On turn 7, the flip's value would need to be an 11 or higher to continue the Encounter; on turn 8, it would be a 12, and so forth.*

Determining a Winner

At the end of an Encounter, players reveal all secret Schemes and add up the VP they earned for completing their Strategies and Schemes. When scoring a Strategy or Scheme, score all victory conditions that apply to you. **A player can score a maximum of 8 VP in Scraps and 10 VP in Brawls. Any VP earned beyond the maximum are ignored. The player with the most VP is the winner. If players are tied for VP, the Encounter is a draw.**

LOCATIONS

Each location entry, whether outdoor or indoor, begins with a brief description of the location, followed by a list of Suggested Terrain with which to populate an Encounter in that location. Consider terrain traits to apply to common terrain features and areas and agree upon these features before play begins (p.58). For example, in a Tavern, the indoor battlefield may have multiple tables and a bar. The table might occupy a 2.5" diameter area and players agree that each table is **Ht** 1, breakable (3), covering terrain. The tavern's bar would follow all the rules of an outdoor fence: **Ht** 1, blocking, severe terrain.

During terrain setup, after a player has flipped for the Encounter location, have another player flip a Fate Card and compare its value to the chosen location's corresponding Location Feature Chart. Depending on the flip, this can result in a special terrain feature with its own special rules being placed on the table and/or a special event occurring during the Encounter that may hamper or help the Crews in their struggle. When the Black Joker is flipped, flip two more cards and apply the values. If either of those flips are duplicated, re-flip one card.

OUTDOOR LOCATIONS

Encounters between Crews can occur just about anywhere. From the upscale streets of Downtown to the inhospitable Badlands, Malifaux provides a wide variety of settings in which Crews can settle their differences.

Hag's Territory

Because the Hag wanders the Bayou, just about any type of terrain is possible for Encounters taking place in her territory.

Suggested Terrain: sandbars (open, severe), forests, water terrain, elevated area.

Flip	Feature
Black Joker	Flip two more Cards
1-2	Dark Omens
3-4	Bog
5-7	Ancient Structure
8-9	Magic Nexus
10-11	Mysterious Effigies
12-13	Foggy
Red Joker	Player's Choice from Hag's Territory list

Gremlin Village

These crude settlements can be found scattered throughout the Bayou, home to both Gremlins and their livestock.

Suggested Terrain: animal pens (soft cover), rubble (severe), huts or other structures (blocking and breakable), soggy patches of ground (severe), forests, water effects.

Flip	Feature
Black Joker	Flip two more Cards
1-2	Disturbing Whispers
3-4	Bog
5-7	Creepy Structure
8-9	Torrential Rains
10-11	Dead Zone
12-13	Scrap Pile
Red Joker	Player's Choice from Gremlin Village list

Bayou's Edge

The area marking the border of the Bayou separates the swamp from nearby towns and hills. Often foggy and rainy, this creepy area has its abandoned buildings as well as forested wilds to hide in.

Suggested Terrain: open and severe ground, single trees and forests, tall reeds (soft cover), water effects, elevations.

Flip	Feature
Black Joker	Flip two more Cards
1-2	Forested
3-4	Creepy Structure
5-7	Torrential Rains
8-9	Graveyard
10-11	Hanging Tree
12-13	Campsite
Red Joker	Player's Choice from Bayou's Edge list

Bogs

Many of the brave souls who have dared the Bayou's dangerous bogs have never been seen again.

Suggested Terrain: large areas of severe terrain, ruins (severe and/or hard cover), hazardous terrain, single element trees and forests, tall plant and reed stands (forests), the occasional dry patch of ground (open and/or elevated).

Flip	Feature
Black Joker	Flip two more Cards
1-2	Hanging Tree
3-4	Soulstone Vein
5-7	Bog
8-9	Mysterious Effigies
10-11	Hazardous Terrain
12-13	Foggy
Red Joker	Player's Choice from Bogs list

Downtown

The downtown area, full of residences and businesses, is the Guild's shining example of what the City could be, given enough time and resources.

Suggested Terrain: walls and fences (blocking and/or covering), buildings, fountains (blocking and/or severe), bridges over dry or water terrain.

Terrain can be climbable or breakable as players see fit.

Flip	Feature
Black Joker	Flip two more Cards
1-2	Graveyard
3-4	Dead Zone
5-7	Heat Wave
8-9	Creepy Structure
10-11	Torrential Rains
12-13	Foggy
Red Joker	Player's Choice from Downtown list

Industrial Zone

The Industrial Zone is home to the majority of Malifaux's factories and industry.

Suggested Terrain: walls (soft and/or hard cover), rubble (severe and/or hard cover), hazardous terrain (blocking), climbable terrain, breakable terrain, water effects.

Flip	Feature
Black Joker	Flip two more Cards
1-2	Hazardous Terrain
3-4	Heat Wave
5-7	Scrap Pile
8-9	Rubble
10-11	Foggy
12-13	Creepy Structure
Red Joker	Player's Choice from Industrial Zone list

Slums

Those not affluent or powerful enough to live Downtown are forced to survive in the dangerous Slums, gathering in the bars, opium dens, brothels, and gambling houses and making their way through ruined buildings, cracked stone plazas, and crooked, winding streets.

Suggested Terrain: walls and fences (blocking and/or covering), ruins (severe and/or covering), fountains (blocking and/or severe), bridges over dry or water terrain.

Terrain should be climbable and/or breakable as players see fit.

Flip	Feature
Black Joker	Flip two more Cards
1-2	Scrap Pile
3-4	Alone in the Dark
5-7	Rubble
8-9	Creepy Structure
10-11	Hanging Tree
12-13	Graveyard
Red Joker	Player's Choice from Slums list

Quarantine Zone

This part of the City has been given over to the rapacious forces threatening the Guild.

Suggested Terrain: rubble (severe), ruins (severe and/or hard cover), hazardous terrain, free-standing walls (blocking terrain), climbable terrain, breakable terrain.

Flip	Feature
Black Joker	Flip two more Cards
1-2	Rubble
3-4	Ancient Monument
5-7	Alone in the Dark
8-9	Magic Nexus
10-11	Foggy
12-13	Disturbing Whispers
Red Joker	Player's Choice from Quarantine Zone list

Ruins

Evidence of a civilization that predates even the City's founders is scattered across Malifaux.

Suggested Terrain: rubble (severe), ruins (severe and/or hard cover), hazardous terrain, free-standing walls (blocking terrain), climbable terrain, breakable terrain, water effects.

Flip	Feature
Black Joker	Flip two more Cards
1-2	Soulstone Vein
3-4	Disturbing Whispers
5-7	Rubble
8-9	Cruel Winds
10-11	Rockfall
12-13	Campsite
Red Joker	Player's Choice from Ruins list

Mine

Mining concerns can be found nearly anywhere in Malifaux, but are most concentrated in the Badlands.

Suggested Terrain: mining equipment (severe, blocking, and or soft/hard cover), hazardous terrain, elevations, ruins (severe and/or hard cover), climbable terrain.

Flip	Feature
Black Joker	Flip two more Cards
1-2	Alone in the Dark
3-4	Magic Nexus
5-7	Soulstone Vein
8-9	Rockfall
10-11	Dead Zone
12-13	Hazardous Terrain
Red Joker	Player's Choice from Mine list

Pioneer Town/Ghost Town

Many successful (and not so successful) expansion towns dot the Badlands.

Suggested Terrain: structures (climbable and/or breakable), walls and fences (soft and/or hard cover), ruins (severe and/or hard cover), rubble (severe), blocking terrain, water effects.

Flip	Feature
Black Joker	Flip two more Cards
1-2	Hanging Tree
3-4	Heat Wave
5-7	Mysterious Effigies
8-9	Dark Omens
10-11	Graveyard
12-13	Heavy Snows
Red Joker	Player's Choice from Pioneer/Ghost Town list

Badlands

The inhospitable Badlands stretches out from the City for hundreds of miles. Life in the Badlands is usually brutal and mercifully short.

Suggested Terrain: large areas of open terrain, cacti (single element and area terrain), hazardous terrain, boulders (hard cover), ruins (severe and/or hard cover), rubble (severe), elevations.

Flip	Feature
Black Joker	Flip two more Cards
1-2	Stampede!
3-4	Soulstone Vein
5-7	Heat Wave
8-9	Forested
10-11	Hazardous Terrain
12-13	Heavy Snows
Red Joker	Player's Choice from Badlands list

Mountains

Crews finding themselves in Malifaux's distant and mysterious mountain ranges quickly learn how unforgiving Nature can be.

Suggested Terrain: elevations, severe terrain, forests, climbable terrain, hazardous terrain, water effects.

Flip	Feature
Black Joker	Flip two more Cards
1-2	Hazardous Terrain
3-4	Ancient Monument
5-7	Rockfall
8-9	Heavy Snows
10-11	Magic Nexus
12-13	Earthquake
Red Joker	Player's Choice from Mountains list

INDOOR LOCATIONS

Malifaux battles occur in the most varied of conditions and Masters have proven themselves necessarily adaptable to conflict in those differing conditions. Marcus has fought in city streets, Leveticus has fought at the Bayou's Edge, and Perdita has fought in the Northern Mountains. Some battles, though, are not fought in the wide open spaces, but in the tighter confines of locations like Colette's Star Theater, or narrow caves, the Qi and Gong tavern, or even Nicodem's Observatory.

Fighting an Encounter at an indoor location is not significantly different from fighting at an outdoor location other than how your terrain setup looks. The most significant change to Encounter play is the walls.

Indoor Walls
- To emulate the enclosed spaces of an indoor location with a solid ceiling, assume all walls (natural and man-made) are **Ht 4** and models with **Flight** or **Float** may not pass over indoor walls.
- Walls that are less than ½" thick are breakable (unless otherwise indicated or agreed upon by players prior to Encounter play) (p.58). A wall's Hardness is determined by the players before the Encounter begins. A model attacking any segment of wall and surpassing its declared Hardness creates a 3" hole through the wall. Mark this section as severe terrain. Each building and/or wall may have a unique Hardness value assigned to it but the suggested Hardness values are: wood: 3, brick: 6, stone/cobblestone: 8, metal: 10.

Large Theater

A chance encounter between two Crews turns this bastion of the arts into a battleground.

Suggested Terrain: Stage is Ht 2 severe terrain, impassable terrain (pipe organ), ½" walls to mark off a 6"x6" back room, crates and barrels (severe , covering).

Flip	Feature
Black Joker	Flip two more Cards
1-2	Bag of Soulstones
3-4	Drink Up!
5-7	Dim Lighting
8-9	Growing Fire
10-11	Pool of Aether
12-13	Hazardous Terrain
Red Joker	Player's Choice from Large Theater list

Sewers

A great labyrinth of connected water channels exists beneath the City and far beyond its borders.

Suggested Terrain: 2"-4" wide water terrain, 1"-3" thick unbreakable walls, severe terrain, blocking terrain, climbable terrain, varying elevations, bridges, impassable terrain.

Flip	Feature
Black Joker	Flip two more Cards
1-2	Caustic Gas
3-4	Flash Flood
5-7	Dim Lighting
8-9	Rubble
10-11	Hazardous Terrain
12-13	Disturbing Whispers
Red Joker	Player's Choice from The Sewers list

Arcanist's Lab

Arcanist laboratories are filled with dangerous apparati and mysterious equipment, some unearthed from ancient ruins and others with an unfathomable foreign origin.

Suggested Terrain: tables (severe, covering, breakable (3)), covering terrain, hazardous terrain, ¼" breakable walls, areas of the table divided into rooms.

Flip	Feature
Black Joker	Flip two more Cards
1-2	Bag of Soulstones
3-4	Recalibration Device
5-7	Pool of Aether
8-9	Ancient Text
10-11	Arcane Apparatus
12-13	Growing Fire
Red Joker	Player's Choice from Arcanist's Lab list

Resurrectionist's Lab

The disturbing and often macabre chambers make the Death Marshals and accompanying Guardsmen regret the discovery.

Suggested Terrain: tables (severe, covering, breakable (3)), covering terrain, hazardous terrain, ¼" breakable walls, areas of the table divided into rooms.

Flip	Feature
Black Joker	Flip two more Cards
1-2	Graveyard
3-4	Ancient Text
5-7	Dim Lighting
8-9	Alone in the Dark
10-11	Torture Chamber
12-13	Mysterious Effigies
Red Joker	Player's Choice from Resurrectionist's Lab list

Guild Library

Serving as a repository for confiscated texts and forgotten Neverborn artifacts, a Guild Library serves as a tempting target for outlaws.

Suggested Terrain: Bookshelves (**Ht** 2 walls, 1" wide, 3-4" long, covering, breakable (3)), tables (severe, covering, breakable (3)), severe terrain, covering terrain, blocking terrain, areas of the table divided into rooms.

Flip	Feature
Black Joker	Flip two more cards
1-2	Pool of Aether
3-4	Dim Lighting
5-7	Cache of Tomes
8-9	Arcane Apparatus
10-11	Disturbing Whispers
12-13	Ancient Text
Red Joker	Player's Choice from Guild Library list

Necropolis

Deep beneath the City and beyond the expansive sewer channels exists an immense system of ancient, connected chambers. None who has sought to explore this network has succeeded, quickly emerging from the sewer system covered in muck, afraid of the shadows forever more. Most are never heard from again.

Suggested Terrain: covering terrain, blocking terrain, climbable terrain, water terrain, the occasional climbable area, areas of the table divided into rooms, impassable terrain.

Flip	Feature
Black Joker	Flip two more Cards
1-2	Disturbing Whispers
3-4	Graveyard
5-7	Ancient Monument
8-9	Magic Nexus
10-11	Alone in the Dark
12-13	Rubble
Red Joker	Player's Choice from Necropolis list

Guild Holding Facility

Beneath the primary Guild offices are many chambers found with solid iron-shod doors. Shackles and chains dangle from secure hooks in the ceiling. The Guild, naturally, uses these chambers as they were originally intended. Escape attempts are common. Success is not.

Suggested Terrain: walls to mark 5"X5" and larger rooms (unbreakable or Hardness 8-10), tables (severe, covering, breakable (3)), blocking terrain.

Flip	Feature
Black Joker	Flip two more Cards
1-2	Dead Zone
3-4	Torture Chamber
5-7	Rubble
8-9	Howling Voices
10-11	Dim Lighting
12-13	Alone in the Dark
Red Joker	Player's Choice from Guild Holding Facility list

Warehouse

Several large buildings are found throughout Malifaux containing great hoards. Guild confiscated items, Arcanist smuggling areas, and Resurrectionist research materials are just the beginning of what can be found by a curious and resourceful Crew.

Suggested Terrain: tables (severe, covering, breakable (3)), severe terrain, blocking terrain, climbable terrain, ¼" breakable walls to create 4"x4" or larger rooms.

Flip	Feature
Black Joker	Flip two more Cards
1-2	Dim Lighting
3-4	Bag of Soulstones
5-7	Scrap Pile
8-9	Growing Fire
10-11	Ancient Text
12-13	Arcane Apparatus
Red Joker	Player's Choice from the Warehouse list

Research Facility

Many different research facilities are found throughout Malifaux. Most are conducted with the Guild's permission and support but some step beyond the line of legality, researching ancient technology and arcane lore. Though their overall purpose might be similar, the contents of these often secret places vary from the mundane to the fantastical.

Suggested Terrain: tables (severe, covering, breakable (3)), ¼" breakable walls to create 4"x4" or larger rooms, hazardous terrain, covering terrain, blocking terrain

Flip	Feature
Black Joker	Flip two more Cards
1-2	Cache of Tomes
3-4	Arcane Apparatus
5-7	Choking Smoke or Gas
8-9	Growing Fire
10-11	Hazardous Terrain
12-13	Recalibration Device
Red Joker	Player's Choice from Research Facility list

Cave/Mine System

Whether a freshly dug mine shaft or the found caves of the Northern Mountains, more and more would-be adventurers ply their trade in the excavation of Soulstone or the sometimes rewarding discoveries of spelunking. Some become so excited by the rich discoveries to be unearthed that they forget where they are: Malifaux, where the darkest tunnels are often filled with the greatest danger.

Suggested Terrain: thick walls (2"-3" thick) , covering terrain, hazardous terrain, impassable terrain, climbable terrain, blocking terrain, water terrain.

Flip	Feature
Black Joker	Flip two more Cards
1-2	Rubble
3-4	Bag of Soulstones
5-7	Dim Lighting
8-9	Hazardous Terrain
10-11	Soulstone Vein
12-13	Rockfall
Red Joker	Player's Choice from Cave/Mine System list

Ancient Ruins

Lost in the overgrown wilderness of the Bayou to the east and scattered through the Northern Hills and Badlands to the west, explorers and adventurers have uncovered crumbled complexes created and abandoned by a very ancient culture.

Suggested Terrain: Walls, areas divided into rooms, blocking terrain, impassable terrain, covering terrain, hazardous terrain, climbable terrain.

Flip	Feature
Black Joker	Flip two more Cards
1-2	Rockfall
3-4	Cache of Tomes
5-7	Ancient Monument
8-9	Howling Voices
10-11	Arcane Apparatus
12-13	Ancient Text
Red Joker	Player's Choice from Ancient Ruins list

Large Tavern

Within the dangerous and dirty section of the Slums, the inhabitants of Malifaux seek solace in their cups. The Qi and Gong and other taverns cater to the various lusts of settlers looking to escape the drudgery of laborious and dangerous workdays and the fear of the unknown perils of the Malifaux wilderness. Fights are common, winners are not.

Suggested Terrain: Thin walls (hardness 2) separate 5"X5" rooms filled with severe, covering, or blocking terrain and tables (severe, covering, breakable (3)).

Flip	Feature
Black Joker	Flip two more Cards
1-2	Bag of Soulstones
3-4	Howling Voices
5-7	Drink Up!
8-9	Dim Lighting
10-11	Wetbar
12-13	Growing Fire
Red Joker	Player's Choice from Large Tavern list

Collapsed City Block

Within the Quarantine Zone and even within the Slums, some buildings have given in to the withering effects of time and dilapidation. Sometimes, brave and resourceful souls scavenging through the debris come out with a treasure or tale worth the risks.

Suggested Terrain: severe terrain, blocking terrain, impassable terrain, walls, hazardous terrain, climbable terrain.

Flip	Feature
Black Joker	Flip two more Cards
1-2	Ancient Text
3-4	Arcane Apparatus
5-7	Rubble
8-9	Hazardous Terrain
10-11	Rockfall
12-13	Dark Omens
Red Joker	Player's Choice from Collapsed City Zone list

*Example: In an Encounter taking place in the Sewers, walls might be 1" thick (unbreakable, and follow the rules for Indoor Walls) and Water Terrain might cover much of the table in narrow 2"-4" wide channels. While most Water features have an Encounter effect of **None**, the sewer water might have the severe trait, or even the hazardous trait (for example: models suffer 1 **Wd** when moving into or ending their activation in sewer water).*

LOCATION FEATURES

Special Terrain

Unless otherwise indicated in the descriptions below, when setting up terrain, a special terrain piece must be placed somewhere outside of the Deployment Zones (p.66), at least 6" from either Deployment Zone. Players should agree on who will place the terrain (or flip for it). The terrain piece can be oriented in any direction when placed on the table.

Reminder:

(#) Interact: The model spends the indicated number of Actions to **Interact** with the Encounter table or object in base contact. *For example: Picking up a bag of Soulstones in a Story scenario is a (1) Interact Action.*

Arcane Apparatus: Each player places a 50mm Marker. A model may **(1) Interact** with the Marker once per turn to Flip a Fate Card. The model adds the suit shown on the Fate Card to its Duel totals. Flipping the Black Joker removes all suits associated with the model's statistics. Flipping the Red Joker allows the model to add any one suit to its Duel totals. The effects of the flip last until the end of the model's next activation.

Ancient Monument: 50mm, **Ht** 5, blocking terrain. Models within 1" of the Ancient Monument receive +1 Ca.

Ancient Text: At the beginning of the Encounter, each player places one Book Counter in base contact with a terrain feature and at least 8" from each Deployment Zone. A model in base contact with the Counter may **(1) Interact** to pick it up. A model carrying a Book Counter gains "**Arcane Reservoir**: Increase this model's Crew's Maximum Hand Size by 1 while it is in play." Before a model carrying a Book Counter leaves play, place the Book Counter in base contact with the model. Models cannot carry more than one Book Counter at any time.

Bag of Soulstones: At the beginning of the Encounter, each player places a Marker on the table, at least 10" away from their Deployment Zone. A model with the **Use Soulstone** Ability may **(1) Interact** with a Marker to discard it and gain two Soulstones.

Bog: For the duration of the Encounter, any portion of the table without a terrain piece receives the severe and water traits.

Cache of Tomes: Players alternate placing a total of six Book Counters on the table, following the Special Terrain setup rules. Book Counters must be placed at least 6" from one another. A model in base contact with a Book Counter may **(1) Interact** to flip a Fate Card. Apply the results of the flip to the model as follows:

Black Joker: **Paralyzed.**

🗡: The model's ⚔ and ⌐ **Strikes** and spells receive +1 **Dg.**

✗: The model gains **Slow to Die** and **Hard to Wound 1.**

🐾: The model gains **Black Blood** and **(+1) Nimble.**

📖: The model gains +1 **Ca** and **Magic Resistant +1.**

Red Joker: Flip twice and apply the effects of both Cards. If the second Card is the same suit as the first, it has no effect.

The effects of this flip last until the end of the model's next activation.

Campsite: Place a 2" X 2" or larger severe terrain feature. A model may **(1) Interact** with the Campsite to discard one Control Card and then draw one Control Card.

Creepy Structure: Place a 3" X 3" or larger terrain feature. A model in base contact with the Creepy Structure may **(1) Interact** once per turn to flip a Fate Card. Apply the results of the flip to the model as follows:

Joker: The model is killed.

1-3: The model suffers 2 **Wd.**

4-6: The model may inflict 2 **Wd** on another model in base contact with the structure.

7-9: The model heals 2 **Wd.**

10-11: This model's Controller's Soulstone pool gains two Soulstones.

12-13: This model's Controller's Soulstone pool gains two Soulstones and the model heals all **Wd.**

Dead Zone: Place a 3"X3" or larger open terrain feature. A model cannot cast spells while in base contact with the Dead Zone.

Drink Up!: At the beginning of the Encounter, select one 1"x5" or larger terrain feature. A model beginning or ending its activation within 1" of the feature may **(1) Interact** with it to make a Healing Flip. The model receives **Slow** and may not take **(0)** Actions during its next activation.

Forested: For the duration of the Encounter, any portion of the table without a terrain piece receives the obscuring trait, and LoS range is reduced to 3".

Graveyard: Place a 3" x 3" or larger terrain feature. A model gains one Corpse Counter when it **(1) Interacts** while its base is completely within the Graveyard. Any tombstones in the terrain feature are considered **Ht** 1, and covering.

Hanging Tree: Place a 50mm, **Ht** 6, blocking terrain feature. The tree is **Terrifying → 12** and has a range of 2".

Hazardous Terrain: Place a 3" X 3" or larger terrain feature. The player placing the hazardous terrain declares what type of hazard the terrain piece is and how much damage the terrain causes. Players should use one of the damage ratings from Terrain (p.59) or agree on a damage rating for the hazard.

Magic Nexus: Place a 3" X 3" terrain feature. The Casting and Resist Flips of models whose bases are completely within the area receive ⊞.

Mysterious Effigies: Each player places two 30mm Markers at least 10" outside of any Deployment Zone and away from any other Mysterious Effigy Marker. At the end of the Encounter, the player with the closest model within 2" of an Effigy Marker scores 1 VP.

Pool of Aether: Place a 3"X3" or larger terrain feature. A model with the **Use Soulstone** Ability whose base is completely within the area may spend one Soulstone per turn without deducting it from its Soulstone Pool.

Rubble: For the duration of the Encounter, any portion of the table without a terrain feature receives the severe trait.

Recalibration Device: Place a 50mm, **Ht** 4 terrain feature. A model may **(1) Interact** while in base contact with the feature to choose one of the following effects below and force a target non-Master Construct model in LoS of the **Recalibration Device** to win a **Wp→15** Duel or gain the chosen effect.

- **(+1) Nimble**
- **(2) Flurry**
- **Slow**
- **Dg** 1/2/4

Wetbar: Place a 3" x 3" or larger terrain feature. A model in base contact with the feature may **(2) Interact** to make two Healing Flips. The model also receives **Slow** and **Easy to Wound 1** until the end of its next activation.

Scrap Pile: Place a 3" x 3" or larger severe terrain feature. A model gains one Scrap Counter when it **(1) Interacts** while its base is completely within the Scrap Pile.

Soulstone Vein: Place a terrain feature no larger than 2" x 2". A Master gains # Soulstone when it **(#) Interacts** while its base is completely within the Soulstone Vein.

Torture Chamber: Place a 3"X3" or larger terrain feature. When a model whose base is completely within the feature kills another model, its controller's Soulstone Pool gains one Soulstone. A model within the feature also gains the **Terrifying→12** Ability if it is not already **Terrifying**.

Special Events

Special events occur during one or more turns of the Encounter. Each event indicates when it takes place during the turn. Events that last until the end of the Encounter begin at the start of the Draw Phase in turn 1.

To determine whether a Random event happens in the following turn, the last player who activated a model flips a Fate Card at the end of the current turn's Closing Phase. If the card is a Joker, 10, 11, 12, or 13, the event occurs; otherwise, no event occurs. Random Events do not occur until the end of the first turn of the Encounter.

Alone in the Dark: Until the end of the Encounter, a model forced to fall back after it loses a Morale Duel is killed instead.

Cruel Winds (Random): At the start of the Encounter, randomly determine a table edge. During the next turn, each model is Pushed 1" toward that table edge at the end of its activation.

Caustic Gas: Until the end of the Encounter, all models receive -1/-1 **Wk/Cg**. All ranged Attack Flips and Casting Flips receive ⊟.

Dark Omens (Random): From the beginning of next turn's Draw Phase to the end of its Activation Phase, Fate Cards with a value of 1 count as value 13 and vice versa.

Dim Lighting: Until the end of the Encounter, LoS cannot be drawn further than 8".

Disturbing Whispers: Until the end of the Encounter, all models receive -1 **Wp** when defending in a Duel.

Earthquake (Random): At the start of the next turn's Activation Phase, each player, in activation order, may Push all of his or her opponents' models 1" in any direction unless those models have **Flight** or **Float**.

Flash Flood (Random): At the start of the Encounter, randomly determine a table edge. During the next turn, models cannot take the **Charge** Action and Push each model 2" toward that table edge at the beginning of its activation.

Foggy (Random): During the next turn, all Attack Flips and Casting Flips receive ⊟.

Growing Fire (Random): At the start of next turn's Draw Phase, the player who activated this event places a 50mm Fire Marker (Ht 5, obscuring, hazardous (2/4/7)) in base contact with a terrain feature no closer than 3" from any model. If the Marker cannot be placed, the event does not occur this turn. Another player then places an additional 50mm Fire Marker touching the first Fire Marker. This Fire Marker can be placed touching or overlapping model bases.

For the remainder of the Encounter, each time this event occurs, the player who activated it places an additional 50mm Fire Marker touching any Fire Marker already in play. After this marker is placed, the next player in activation order also places a Fire Marker. Any of these Fire Markers can be placed touching or overlapping model bases.

Heat Wave (Random): During the next turn, models receive -1/-1 **Wk/Cg**.

Heavy Snows (Random): During the next turn, models cannot **Charge** and receive -2 **Cb** to ranged **Strikes** and -2 **Cb** to Spells with the ⌐ icon. Models with **Frozen Heart** or **Smoldering Heart** are immune to Heavy Snows.

Howling Voices (Random): During the next turn, models cannot activate simultaneously and all models receive -2 **Ca** when targeting another model with a Spell.

Rockfall (Random): At the start of the next turn's Activation Phase, any model within 1" of a terrain feature immediately suffers 1 **Wd**.

Stampede! (Random): At the start of the next turn's Activation Phase, all models within 8" of the centerline immediately suffer a number of **Wd** equal to their **Ht**.

Torrential Rains (Random): During the next turn, models cannot **Charge**.

COMPLETE STRATEGIES LIST

Simple Strategies

A Line in the Sand

You're tired of your opponent invading your turf, so you're going to draw a line in the sand... with dynamite.

Setup
Place five 30mm Dynamite Markers along the centerline of the table at least 6" apart.

Special
The Dynamite Markers begin the Encounter Disarmed. Your models may take a **(1) Interact** Action while in base contact with a Dynamite Marker to Arm it. Your opponent's models may take a **(2) Interact** Action while in base contact with an Armed Dynamite Marker to Disarm it. Insignificant models and models engaged with enemy models cannot take either of these Actions.

Victory
If at least three Dynamite Markers are Armed at the end of the Encounter, you score **2 VP**.
OR
If all five Dynamite Markers are Armed at the end of the Encounter, you score **4 VP**.

Claim Jump

Time to stake your claim in someone else's territory!

Setup
Place a 30mm Claim Marker at least 8" away from the center of the table and at least 12" from your Deployment Zone.

Special
Insignificant models do not count toward the Victory condition.

Victory
If you have more models completely within 3" of the Claim Marker than your opponent does at the end of the Encounter, you score **2 VP**.
OR
If you have twice as many or more models completely within 3" of the Claim Marker than your opponent does at the end of the Encounter, you score **4 VP**.

Contain Power

You have been assigned to contain the expansion of your opponent's power.

Victory
If all of your opponent's leaders are no longer in the game at the end of the Encounter, you score **2 VP**.
OR
If all of your opponent's leaders are no longer in the game at the end of the Encounter and were either killed or sacrificed by your leaders, you score **4 VP**.

Deliver a Message

I'm just the messenger!

Special

A model in your Crew may make a **(2) Interact** Action while within 2" of one of your opponents' leaders to Deliver a Message. Insignificant models cannot take this Action.

Victory

If one of your models Delivers the Message while within 2" of an opposing leader during the Encounter, you score **2 VP.**

OR

If one of your models Delivers the Message while within 2" of an opposing leader during the first four turns of the Encounter, you score **4 VP.**

Destroy the Evidence

The opposing Crew has stumbled upon potentially damning evidence your Crew would prefer didn't exist. Destroy the evidence before it's too late!

Setup

Place one 30mm Evidence Marker completely inside your opponent's Deployment Zone and two 30mm Evidence Markers completely within 10" of your opponent's Deployment Zone. These Markers must be placed at least 8" from one another.

Special

Your models in base contact with an Encounter Marker may take a **(1) Interact** Action to Destroy the Evidence and remove the Marker from the game. Insignificant models and models engaged with enemy models cannot take this Action.

Victory

If at least two of the Evidence Markers have been removed from the game by the end of the Encounter, you score **2 VP.**

OR

If all three of the Evidence Markers have been removed from the game by the end of the Encounter, you score **4 VP.**

Distract

Keep your opponent busy elsewhere long enough to miss the real fireworks!

Special

Insignificant models do not count toward the Victory condition.

Victory

If your opponent does not have any leaders completely in your Deployment Zone at the end of the Encounter, you score **2 VP.**

OR

If your opponent does not have any leaders completely on your half of the table at the end of the Encounter, you score **4 VP.**

Escape and Survive

Discretion is the better part of valor...at least you hope it is.

Setup

Note the number of models in your Crew at the start of the Encounter.

Special

Insignificant models <u>do</u> count toward the Setup or Victory condition. Summoned models do not count toward the Victory condition unless another friendly model was killed or sacrificed when Summoning the model.

Victory

If you have at least 50% of the number of models you started the Encounter with in play at the end of the Encounter and those models are at least 8" from your Deployment Zone, you score **2 VP.**

OR

If you have at least 75% of the number of models you started the Encounter with in play at the end of the Encounter and those models are at least 8" from your Deployment Zone, you score **4 VP.**

Plant Evidence

You've decided to try to turn public opinion against your opponents by framing them, but to do this you need to plant the evidence.

Special

A model in your Crew may take a **(1) Interact** Action to Plant Evidence when in base contact with a piece of terrain completely on its opponent's side of the table. You may not Plant Evidence on the same piece of terrain more than once during the Encounter. Insignificant models and models engaged with enemy models cannot take this Action.

Victory

If your models Planted Evidence on at least two pieces of terrain completely on your opponent's half of the table during the Encounter, you score **2 VP.**

OR

If your models Planted Evidence on at least four pieces of terrain completely on your opponent's half of the table, or on at least two pieces of terrain in the opponent's Deployment Zone during the Encounter, you score **4 VP.**

Reconnoiter

Investigate the surrounding area.

Setup
Divide the table into equal quarters.

Special
Insignificant models and models within 3" of the center of the table do not count toward the Victory condition. You control a table quarter when the majority of models completely within that quarters are yours.

Victory
If you have control of at least three table quarters at the end of the Encounter, you score **2 VP.**

OR

If you have control of all four table quarters at the end of the Encounter, you score **4 VP.**

Slaughter

They've gone too far. Time to wipe them out.

Special
Each time a player kills or sacrifices an enemy model during the Encounter, that player notes its Soulstone Cost. Masters are worth 10 Soulstones for the purpose of this Strategy (multiple model Masters such as The Dreamer and Viktoria are worth 6 Soulstones per model). Models that are Summoned into play and killed will add their Soulstone costs. Models with no Soulstone cost who enter play by replacing another model(s) are worth the Soulstone cost of the model(s) they replaced. Models that can return to play, when killed for the first time by the opposing player, count their Soulstones only the first time they are killed.

Victory
If the total Soulstone Cost of enemy models you have killed or sacrificed is greater than the total Soulstone Cost of your models your opponent has killed or sacrificed, you score **2 VP.**

OR

If the total Soulstone Cost of enemy models you have killed or sacrificed is 1.5 times the total Soulstone Cost of your models your opponent has killed or sacrificed, you score **4 VP.**

Supply Wagon

You are transporting some vital supplies, and they must arrive intact!

Setup
Place a 50mm Wagon Marker (**Ht** 4, impassable, hardness 3, and can suffer 3 **Dg** before being removed from the game) completely within your Deployment Zone and touching a table edge in your Deployment Zone after all Crews are deployed.

Special
Each turn, move the Wagon Marker 6" toward the center of the table at the start of the Resolve Effects Step. The Marker may not move over models and stops if it comes in contact with them. Models may attack the Wagon Marker with melee attacks only. The Marker cannot be attacked if it is within the melee range of one of your models.

Victory
If the Wagon Marker is completely within 3" of the center of the table at the end of the Encounter but has suffered 1 or more Dg, you score **2 VP.**

OR

If the Wagon Marker is completely within 3" of the center of the table at the end of the Encounter and has suffered 0 Dg, you score **4 VP.**

Treasure Hunt

You have discovered the location of a valuable artifact and must take possession of it.

Setup
Place a 30mm Treasure Counter in the center of the table.

Special
Your models in base contact with the Treasure Counter may take a **(1) Interact** Action to pick it up. A model carrying the Counter can drop or pass it to another model in base contact as a **(1) Interact** Action. Models controlled by your opponent can take this Action once one of your models has picked up the Counter at least once during the Encounter.

A model changing position on the table by an effect other than the **Walk** Action or leaving play drops the Treasure Counter in base contact with itself. While carrying the Counter, a model reduces its **Wk** to 4, and cannot have its **Wk** increased by any means. Spirits lose the ability to move through other models and the ability to ignore terrain penalties while carrying the Treasure Counter. Models lose **Flight** or **Float** while carrying the Treasure Counter.

The Treasure Counter does not count as being carried if carried by an Insignificant model at the end of the Encounter.

Victory
At the end of the Encounter, if the Treasure Counter is carried by one of your models but not in your Deployment Zone or is completely within your Deployment Zone but not carried by a model, you score **2 VP**.
OR
If the Treasure Counter is carried by one of your models and that model is completely within your Deployment Zone at the end of the Encounter, you score **4 VP**.

Turf War

You wish to claim a little of your opponent's real estate for yourself.

Special
Insignificant models do not count toward the Victory condition.

Victory
If you have more of your models completely on your opponent's half of the table than they have models completely on your half of the table at the end of the Encounter, you score **2 VP**.
OR
If you have more of your models completely on your opponent's half of the table than they have models completely on your half of the table and you have at least one model completely within their Deployment Zone at the end of the Encounter, you score **4 VP**.

Shared Strategies List

With Shared Strategies, multiple players may earn VP if they accomplish the required tasks.

Shared A Line in the Sand

They've drawn the line, not you. Why don't you use some fireworks to show them how little that line will slow your ambitions?

Setup
After selecting this Strategy, both players flip a Card. The player with the high card decides if he or she would like to be the Attacker or Defender. If the flips are tied, re-flip until one player has the high card.

The Attacker places five 30mm Dynamite Markers along the center line of the table, at least 6" apart.

Special
The Dynamite Markers begin the Encounter Disarmed. A model in the Attacking Crew may take a **(1) Interact** Action while in base contact with a Dynamite Marker to Arm it. A model in the Defending Crew may make an **(2) Interact** Action while in base contact with an armed Dynamite Marker to Disarm it. Insignificant models or models engaged with an enemy model cannot take these Actions.

Victory
Attacker:
If at least two Dynamite Markers are Armed at the end of the Encounter, you score **2 VP**. For each additional Dynamite Marker over three Armed at the end of the Encounter, you score **+1 VP**.

Defender:
If at least three Dynamite Markers are Disarmed at the end of the Encounter, you score **2 VP**. For each additional Dynamite Marker over three Disarmed at the end of the Encounter, you score **+1 VP**.

Shared Claim Jump

Time to stake your claim in someone else's territory!

Setup
Place a 30mm Claim Marker in the center of the table.

Special
Insignificant models do not count toward the Victory condition.

Victory
If a player has more models completely within 3" of the Claim Marker than his or her opponent does at the end of the Encounter, that player scores **2 VP**.
If that player's opponent does not have any models completely within 3" of the Claim Marker at the end of the Encounter, he or she scores **+2 VP**.

Shared Contain Power

Both Masters have watched their opponents gain too much influence and too strong a foothold in Malifaux.

Victory

A player scores **2 VP** if all of his or her opponent's leaders are no longer in the game at the end of the Encounter.

That player scores **+2 VP** if his or her leaders killed or sacrificed all of the opponent's leaders.

Shared Deliver a Message

I'm just the messenger!

Special

A model in your Crew may take a **(2) Interact** Action while within 2" of one of your opponents' leaders to Deliver a Message. Insignificant models cannot take this Action.

Victory

If a player's model Delivers the Message during the Encounter, that player scores **1 VP**.

That player scores **+1 VP** if the Message was Delivered during the first four turns of the Encounter.

That player scores **+2 VP** if his or her Message was Delivered before the opponent's was.

Shared Destroy the Evidence

"The opposing Crew has come into possession of some potentially damning information your Crew would prefer didn't exist. Destroy the evidence before it's too late!"

Setup

Each player places one 30mm Evidence Marker completely inside his or her opponent's Deployment Zone and two Evidence Markers completely within 10" of his or her opponent's Deployment Zone. These Markers must be placed at least 8" from one another. Place an additional neutral Evidence Marker at the center of the table.

Special

A friendly model in base contact with an Evidence Marker that you placed may take a **(2) Interact** Action to Destroy the Evidence and remove the Marker from the game. Any model in base contact with the neutral Evidence Marker may take a **(2) Interact** Action to Destroy the Evidence and remove the Marker from the game. Insignificant models and models engaged with enemy models cannot take this Action.

Victory

A player scores **+1 VP** if his or her Crew Destroys both the Evidence Markers that he or she placed outside an opponent's Deployment Zone.

A player scores **+2 VP** if his or her Crew Destroys the Evidence Marker he or she placed in an opponent's Deployment Zone.

A player scores **+1 VP** if his or her Crew Destroys the neutral Evidence Marker.

Shared Distract

Keep your opponent busy elsewhere long enough to miss the real fireworks!

Special
Insignificant models do not count toward the Victory condition.

Victory
If a player's opponent does not have any leaders completely in the player's deployment zone at the end of the Encounter, that player scores **2 VP**.
If that player's opponent also has no opposing leaders completely on the player's half of the table at the end of the Encounter, that player scores **+2 VP**.

Shared Escape and Survive

Neither of you can afford any more losses right now.

Setup
Note the number of models in your Crew at the start of the Encounter.

Special
Insignificant models <u>do</u> count toward the Setup or Victory condition. Summoned models do not count toward the victory condition unless another friendly model was killed or sacrificed when Summoning the model.

Victory
If a player has at least 50% of the number of models he or she started the Encounter with in play at the end of the Encounter and those models are at least 8" from his or her Deployment Zone, that player scores **2 VP**.
If that player has at least 75% of the number of models he or she started the Encounter with in play at the end of the Encounter and those models are at least 8" from his or her Deployment Zone, that player scores **+1 VP**.
The player who has lost the fewest number of models scores **+1 VP**.

Shared Plant Evidence

You've decided to try to turn public opinion against your opponents by framing them, but to do this you need to plant the evidence.

Special
A model may take a **(1) Interact** Action to Plant Evidence when in base contact with a terrain feature on its opponent's half of the table. You may not Plant Evidence on the same piece of terrain more than once during the Encounter. A model cannot take this Action if it is Insignificant or engaged with an enemy model.

Victory
A player scores **1 VP** for each piece of Evidence his or her models Planted on terrain completely on an opponent's half of the table up to a maximum of **4 VP**.

Shared Reconnoiter

Each of you have decided to investigate the surrounding area in an effort to learn more about it than your opponent.

Setup
Divide the table into equal quarters.

Special
Insignificant models and models within 3" of the center of the table do not count toward the Victory condition. You control a table quarter when the majority of models completely within that quarter are yours.

Victory
A player scores **1 VP** for each table quarter he or she controls at the end of the Encounter.

Shared Slaughter

Only one of us walks away from this...

Special
Each time a player kills or sacrifices an enemy model during the Encounter, that player notes its Soulstone Cost. Masters are worth 10 Soulstones for the purpose of this Strategy (multiple model Masters such as The Dreamer and Viktoria are worth 6 Soulstones per model). Models that are Summoned into play and killed will add their Soulstone costs. Models with no Soulstone cost who enter play by replacing another model(s) are worth the Soulstone cost of the model(s) they replaced. Models that can return to play, when killed for the first time by the opposing player, count their Soulstones only the first time they are killed.

Victory
A player scores **1 VP** if the total Soulstone Cost of enemy models he or she killed or sacrificed is greater than the total Soulstone Cost of his or her models an opponent has killed or sacrificed. That player scores **+1 VP** if the total was 1.5 times that of his or her opponent.

A player scores **+1 VP** if his or her opponent has no leaders in the game at the end of the Encounter. If the total Soulstone Cost of a player's opponent's models still in play at the end of the Encounter is less than half the total Soulstone Cost of his or her Crew at the start of the Encounter that player scores **+1 VP**.

Shared Supply Wagon

Get your supplies through, stop the opponent from doing the same. Simple, eh?

Setup
Each player places a 50mm Wagon Marker (**Ht** 4, impassable, hardness 3, and can suffer 3 **Dg** before being removed from the game) completely within his or her Deployment Zone and touching a table edge in the Deployment Zone after all Crews are deployed.

Special
Each turn, both players move their Wagon Markers 6" toward the center of the table at the start of the Resolve Effects Step. A Wagon Marker may not move over models and stops if it comes in contact with them. Models may attack Wagon Markers with melee attacks only. The Marker cannot be attacked if it is within the melee range of one of its Crew's models.

Victory
If a player's Wagon Marker is completely within 3" of the center of the table at the end of the Encounter and his or her opponent's is not, that player scores **2 VP**.

If a player damages an opponent's Wagon Marker during the Encounter, that player scores **+1 VP**.

If a player's Wagon Marker is undamaged at the end of the Encounter, that player scores **+1 VP**.

Shared Treasure Hunt

Both you and your opponent have uncovered the location of an important Malifaux artifact, and must race to be the first to claim it.

Setup
Place one 30mm Treasure Counter in the center of the table after Crews have deployed, but before the Encounter begins.

Special
A model in base contact with the Treasure Counter may take a **(2) Interact** Action to pick up the Treasure Counter. A model carrying the Counter can drop or pass it to another model in base contact as a **(1) Interact** Action.

A model changing position on the table by an effect other than the **Walk** Action or leaving play drops the Treasure Counter in base contact with itself. While carrying the Counter, a model reduces its **Wk** to 4 and cannot have its **Wk** increased by any means. Spirits lose the ability to move through other models and the ability to ignore terrain penalties while carrying the Treasure Counter. Models lose **Flight** or **Float** while carrying the Treasure Counter.

The Treasure Counter does not count as being carried if carried by an Insignificant model at the end of the Encounter.

Victory
A player scores **2 VP** if, at the end of the Encounter, the Treasure Counter is carried by one of his or her models but is not in his or her Deployment Zone or is completely within his or her Deployment Zone but not carried by a model.

A player scores **4 VP** if the Treasure Counter is carried by one of his or her models and that model is completely within his or her Deployment Zone at the end of the Encounter.

Shared Turf War

You each wish to claim a little of your opponent's real estate for yourself.

Special
Insignificant models do not count toward the Victory condition.

Victory
A player with models completely within his or her opponent's Deployment Zone scores **2 VP**.
The player that has more models completely within his or her opponent's Deployment Zone scores **+1 VP**.
The player that has more models completely within his or her opponent's half of the table scores **+1 VP**.

Schemes List

General Schemes

Assassinate

Your opponent's leadership must die at all costs!

Setup

Secretly make note of one of your opponent's Masters or Henchmen. This Scheme may be taken more than once, but you must choose a different model each time.

Special

You cannot select this Scheme if your Strategy is Contain Power or Shared Contain Power.

Victory

If the noted model is not in the game at the end of the Encounter, you score **1 VP**.

Announced: +1 VP.

Bodyguard

Your Crew's leadership must be protected at all costs!

Special

Secretly make note of one of your Crew's Masters or Henchmen. This Scheme may be taken more than once, but you must choose a different model each time. Multiple model Leaders are considered to be one selection in regards to this Scheme.

Victory

If the noted model was not removed from the game and is in play at the end of the Encounter, you score **1 VP**.

Announced: +1 VP.

Breakthrough

Your Crew must push its way through the opposition.

Special

Insignificant models do not count toward the Victory condition.

Victory

If you have more models in your opponent's Deployment Zone than he or she does at the end of the Encounter, you score **1 VP**.

Announced: +1 VP.

Extermination

Your Crew's sights are fixed on one exterminating one threat.

Special

Select one of the following characteristics at least three of your opponent's models share: Beast, Construct, Doll, Family, Gremlin, Guardsman, Living, Nightmare, Pig, Spirit, Undead, Woe; then note all the models in his or her Crew with that characteristic. This Scheme must be announced.

Victory

If your opponent has no models with the selected characteristic in the game at the end of the Encounter, you score **2 VP**.

Eye for an Eye

It's time to show the opposing Crew you can trade blow for blow when they come a'calling!

Special

Insignificant models do not count toward the Victory condition.

Victory

If the number of models you and your opponent have in play at the end of the Encounter is equal or differs by one model, you score **1 VP**.
Announced: +1 VP.

Frame for Murder

Never hurts to get a little blood on the hands of your rivals...well, it hurts the person providing the blood.

Special

Secretly note one non-Master model in your Crew.

Victory

If the noted model was killed or sacrificed by an opposing Master during the Encounter, you score **1 VP**.
Announced: +1 VP.

Grudge

One of your opponent's Minions rubs you the wrong way.

Special

Secretly note one of your opponent's Minions.

Victory

If the noted Minion was killed by one of your non-Master models' melee Strikes or melee Spells, you score **1 VP**.
Announced: +1 VP.

Hold Out

Stand firm against the enemy.

Special

Insignificant models do not count toward the Victory condition.

Victory

If there are no enemy models completely within your Deployment Zone at the end of the Encounter, you score **1 VP**.
Announced: +1 VP.

Kill Protégée

You've heard that one your opponent's Minions is being groomed as the Master's new Henchman.

Special

Secretly note your opponent's Minion model with the highest Soulstone Cost. If there is a tie for highest Soulstone Cost, secretly select and note one of the tied models.

Victory

If one of your models killed the noted Minion, you score **1 VP**.
Announced: +1 VP.

Stake a Claim

This is your territory, and you'll be damned if some other Crew is going to come in and grab it without a fight!

Special

Make note of a piece of terrain completely on the opponent's half of the table. Insignificant models do not count toward the Victory condition.

Victory

If at least one of your models is in base contact with the piece of terrain at the end of the Encounter, you score **1 VP**.
Announced: +1 VP.

Steal Relic

Your opponent's Master is carrying something you desperately need for your plans!

Special

Your models may take a **(1) Interact** Action while engaged with your opponent's Master and conduct a **Wp→Wp** Duel with the Master to Steal the Relic. Once one of your models Steals the Relic, the **Interact** Action can no longer be taken. Insignificant models cannot take this Action. This Scheme must be announced.

Victory

If one of your models Stole the Relic by the end of the Encounter, you score **1 VP**.
If that model is also in play at the end of the Encounter, you score **+1 VP**.

Faction Specific Schemes

Round Up (Guild Only)

Time to round up the little guys, and leave the big problems for later.

Victory

If your opponent does not have any Minion models in play at the end of the Encounter, you score **1 VP**.
Announced: +1 VP.

Raid! (Guild Only)

Sometimes the Malifaux rabble needs a firm reminder who the law is this side of the Breach. Teach them a lesson.

Victory

If you have more non-Totem Minions in play than your opponent does at the end of the Encounter, you score **1 VP**.
Announced: +1 VP.

Army of the Dead (Resurrectionists Only)

"Raising" an army takes on an entirely different meaning for you.

Special
This Scheme must be announced.

Victory
If the number of Corpse Counters on the table or carried by your models is greater than the number of models your opponent has in play at the end of the Encounter, you score **1 VP**. You score **+1 VP** if the number of Corpse Counters carried by your models is greater than the number of models your opponent has in play at the end of the Encounter.

Death After Death (Resurrectionists Only)

Your Crew only gets larger as the battle rages on.

Special
Note the number of models in your Crew. This Scheme must be announced.

Victory
If you have more models in play at the end of the Encounter than you did at the start of the Encounter, you score **2 VP**.

Power Ritual (Arcanists Only)

You need to set up a complex ritual; get it done – fast!

Special
Your models may take a **(1) Interact** Action to Perform the Ritual when they are within 8" of a table corner. Insignificant models cannot take this Action. This Scheme must be announced.

Victory
If your models Performed the Ritual in three of the four corners of the table during the Encounter, you score **1 VP**.
OR
If your models Performed the Ritual in all four corners of the table during the Encounter, you score **2 VP**.

Sabotage (Arcanists Only)

A little sabotage causes no end of trouble for the opposition, and your Crew excels at it.

Setup
Secretly note a terrain feature completely on the opponent's half of the table.

Special
Models in your Crew may take a **(1) Interact** Action to Sabotage the terrain. Insignificant models cannot take this Action.

Victory
If the Sabotaging model is still in play at the end of the turn it Sabotaged the terrain piece, reveal this Scheme and score **1 VP**.
Announced: +1 VP.

Kidnap (Neverborn Only)

The residents of Malifaux tell stories about your Crew sweeping in and spiriting away its victims during the night. How right they are!

Special

Secretly note three of your opponent's Minions.

Victory

If at least two of the noted models are not in the game at the end of the Encounter, you score **1 VP.**

OR

If all three of the noted models are not in the game at the end of the Encounter, you score **2 VP.**

Reclaim Malifaux (Neverborn Only)

Reclaim Malifaux for the Neverborn!

Setup

Divide the table into nine equal sections as shown in the example to the right.

Special

Your models may take a **(1) Interact** Action while within 1" of a terrain feature to Reclaim a part of Malifaux. Insignificant models or models engaged with an enemy model cannot take this Action. Place a Token on the terrain feature to indicate it has been Reclaimed. Both the terrain feature and the model's base must be completely within the table section the model wishes to Reclaim. This Scheme must be announced.

Victory

If you have Reclaimed at least six table sections at the end of the Encounter, you score **1 VP.**

OR

If you have Reclaimed all nine table sections at the end of the Encounter, you score **2 VP.**

Thwart (Outcasts Only)

Sometimes, preventing the opposition from winning is reward enough...

Special

You may not announce this Scheme.

Victory

Score **1 VP** if your opponent does not announce any Schemes.

Or

Score **2 VP** if your opponent does not earn VP for any of his or her Schemes.

Gather Soulstones (Outcasts Only)

Making it out alive isn't nearly as fun as making it out rich.

Victory

If you have more Soulstones in your Soulstone Pool at the end of the Encounter than your opponent does in his or hers, you score **1 VP.**

Announced: +1 VP.

Master Specific Schemes

Lay These Souls to Rest (Lady Justice Only)

"The souls of the innocent deserve peace. My Judge, we must lay these souls to rest."
— Lady Justice

Special

When an enemy Master or Henchman is killed, place a Restless Soul Counter in base contact with that model before it is removed from play. Lady Justice may sacrifice these Counters using her **Last Rites** Action. You cannot choose this Scheme if your Strategy is Contain Power or Shared Contain Power or combined with the Assassinate Scheme. This Scheme must be announced.

Victory

If all Restless Soul Counters have been removed from play using **Last Rites** and there are no enemy Masters or Henchmen in the game, you score **2 VP**.

Subjugate (Sonnia Criid Only)

"Your will is broken and your body is beyond repair. You have reaped what you have sown and now you must face the consequences. Your servitude will continue until your death." — Sonnia Criid

Special

This Scheme must be announced.

Victory

If Sonnia Criid Summoned two Witchling Stalkers by casting the **Violation of Magic** Spell on two enemy models during the Encounter, you score **2 VP**.

Family Justice (Perdita Ortega Only)

"It's not that I have a bullet with your name on it... it's that I have so many bullets in need of a good home" — Perdita Ortega

Special

This Scheme must be announced.

Victory

If Perdita Ortega killed at least three enemy models while using **Execute** during the Encounter, you score **2 VP**.

Machine Spirit (C. Hoffman Only)

"I prefer machines. They wouldn't betray me." — C. Hoffman

Special

You cannot choose this Scheme if your Strategy is Contain Power or Shared Contain Power or combined with the Assassinate Scheme. This Scheme must be announced.

Victory

If an opposing Master or Henchman was killed by a model you controlled with the **Machine Puppet** Action by the end of the Encounter, you score **2 VP**.

My Little Friend (Seamus, the Mad Hatter Only)

"I don't encourage him to be so bloodthirsty. He just wants to make me proud." – Seamus

Special

You cannot choose this Scheme if your Strategy is Contain Power or Shared Contain Power or combined with the Assassinate Scheme. This Scheme must be announced.

Victory

If your Copycat Killer killed an enemy model with a Soulstone Cost of 7 or more, an enemy Master, or an enemy Henchman during the Encounter, you score **2 VP.**

Surrounded by Death (Nicodem, the Undertaker Only)

"I do not need to animate the dead in order to subjugate my enemy. Sometimes the threat itself is enough to scatter his wits." – Nicodem

Special

This Scheme must be announced.

Setup

Divide the table into equal quarters.

Victory

If each table quarter contains at least one Corpse Counter on the table that is not within 1" of an enemy model at the end of the Encounter, you score **2 VP.**

That One's a Keeper (Dr. Douglas McMourning Only)

"Everyone is not created equal. Their parts aren't either." – McMourning

Special

This Scheme must be announced.

Victory

If McMourning gained at least five Body Part Counters from enemy Masters, Henchmen, or Totems during the Encounter, you score **2 VP.**

Betrayed by Spirits (Kirai Ankoku Only)

"I have no use for the bodies. It is the souls that provide the real strength." – Kirai

Special

You cannot choose this Scheme if your Strategy is Contain Power or Shared Contain Power or combined with the Assassinate Scheme. This Scheme must be announced.

Victory

If at least one opposing Master or Henchman was killed by a friendly Ikiryo, you score **2 VP.**

Do I Have To Do Everything Myself? (Ramos Only)

"Sometimes you have to get a little dirty." – Ramos

Special

This Scheme must be announced.

Victory

If Ramos killed an enemy model with a Clockwork Fist **Strike** and another enemy model with the **Electrical Fire** Spell during the Encounter, you score **2 VP.**

Reflections of December (Rasputina Only)

"I will bring upon them such a cold that the very air will freeze." – Rasputina

Special

This Scheme must be announced.

Victory

If Rasputina killed at least three enemy models with Spells cast using the **Ice Mirror** Ability, you score **2 VP.**

Primal Source (Marcus Only)

"We all must face the Beast Within. We are, after all, animals at heart." – Marcus

Special

This Scheme must be announced.

Victory

If at least two enemy models that gained the Beast characteristic during the Encounter were removed from the game while they had the Beast characteristic, you score **2 VP.**

Perfect Performance (Colette Du Bois Only)

"I'd say you caught me at my best dear, but I don't do off nights." – Collete

Special

This Scheme must be announced.

Victory

If your Crew has seven or more Soulstones in its Soulstone Pool at the end of the Encounter, you score **2 VP.**

A Mother's Love (Lilith, Mother of Monsters Only)

"They need the blood to grow. I just like the taste." – Lilith

Special

This Scheme must be announced.

Victory

If Lilith carries at least four Blood Counters at the end of the Encounter, you score **2 VP.**

Spread Madness (Pandora Only)

"Sometimes the only thing you can do in the face of madness is run." – Sonnia Criid

Special

You cannot choose this Scheme if your Strategy is Contain Power or Shared Contain Power or combined with the Assassinate Scheme. This Scheme must be announced.

Victory

If Pandora kills an enemy Master or Henchman model with the **Self-Loathing** Spell during the Encounter, you score **2 VP**.

Seeds of Betrayal (Zoraida, the Hag Only)

"My little poppets are the cutest little darlings. Say...this one looks a bit like you." – Zoraida

Special

You cannot choose this Scheme if your Strategy is Contain Power or Shared Contain Power or combined with the Assassinate Scheme. This Scheme must be announced.

Victory

If an opposing Master or Henchman was killed by an enemy model you controlled with the **Obey** Spell by the end of the Encounter, you score **2 VP**.

A Bump in the Night (The Dreamer Only)

"I like to play games. Wanna play 'Hide and Seek'? You hide. I'll get'cha!" – The Dreamer

Special

This Scheme must be announced.

Victory

If your Crew killed at least two enemy models while there were no friendly Minions in play, you score **2 VP**.

Soulless Life
(Leveticus, Steampunk Necromancer Only)

"There's a great power in death. Coming back once you know how to do it isn't the problem. It's the going that's such a bear." – Leveticus

Special

You cannot choose this Scheme combined with the Bodyguard Scheme. This Scheme must be announced.

Victory

If Leveticus has been killed or sacrificed in at least four turns during the Encounter and is still in play at the end of the Encounter, you score **2 VP**.

First Blood (Viktoria Only)

"I don't make money until the job gets done, so why wait to get started?" – Viktoria

Special

This Scheme must be announced.

Victory

If the first two models killed during the Encounter were models in enemy Crews, you score **2 VP**.

Pig Food (Som'er Teeth Jones Only)

"Damn pigs!" – Som'er Teeth Jones

Special

This Scheme must be announced.

Victory

If Som'er Teeth Jones Summoned at least two Piglets using the **"Come and Get It!"** Trigger when killing enemy models during the Encounter, you score **2 VP**.

Plague on Malifaux (Hamelin the Plagued Only)

"The teeming rats and festering maggots are not harbingers of the End. Rather, they herald the beginning. " – Hamelin

Special

This Scheme must be announced.

Victory

If by the end of the Encounter at least four Malifaux Rats were Summoned by Hamelin's **Voracious Rats** Ability from enemy models killed by Hamelin's Crew, you score **2 VP**.

COMMON ABILITIES

Arachnid
This model ignores severe and climbable terrain penalties and treats all vertical surfaces as having the climbable trait.

Armor +#
Reduce the **Dg** this model suffers by the indicated number (#) down to a minimum of 1 **Dg**. This is cumulative with any other type of **Armor**.

Black Blood
(☠)1. All non-Neverborn models suffer 1 **Wd** when this model suffers **Wd** from a Melee **Strike** or Melee Spell (⚔).

Bulletproof
This model gains **Armor +#** vs. ranged attacks.

(+1) Casting Expert
This model receives one additional specific AP (p.33) during its activation that can only be used for **Cast** Actions. This Ability does not stack with Casting Master. This Ability is listed under a model's Actions in its description and on its stat card.

(+2) Casting Master
This model receives two additional specific APs (p.33) during its activation that can only be used for **Cast** Actions. This Ability does not stack with Casting Expert. This Ability is listed under a model's Actions in its description and on its stat card.

Comes Cheap
This model's Soulstone Cost is not increased when it is hired by another Faction.

Companion (Model or Characteristic)
Before activating a model with Companion, nominate any number of the referenced model(s) or model(s) with the corresponding Characteristic within 6" of one another. These models activate simultaneously. Choose one of the nominated models to activate first, and complete its entire activation. Then the Controller chooses and activates another nominated model. Continue activating the nominated models until all nominated models have completed their activations.

COMPANION DIAGRAM:
It's Casey's turn to activate a model. Looking at her models, she sees that Perdita and Niño are within 6" of one another and Papa Loco is within 6" of Niño. She announces that she is activating all three of the models via Companion. She then chooses to complete Papa's activation first; next, she chooses to complete Perdita's activation; and finally, she completes Niño's.

Easy to Wound

Damage Flips against this model receive one 🔱 per indicated number (#).

Evasive

This model gains **Armor +#** vs. ♣.

Float

This model may move over terrain and other models without penalty, and can end its movement on impassable terrain but cannot end its movement overlapping another model's base. When this model moves, it is immune to disengaging **Strikes** from all models except those that it was engaged in melee with when it began its movement.

Flight

This model may move over terrain and other models without penalty but it cannot end its movement on impassable terrain and cannot end its movement overlapping another model's base. When this model moves, it is immune to disengaging **Strikes** from all models except those that it was engaged in melee with when it began its movement.

Gunfighter [Weapon]

This model can make melee **Strikes** against enemy models up to 2" away with the indicated ranged Weapon. The indicated Weapon gains 🗡 and loses ➳ when making these **Strikes**. Models with this Ability can block disengaging models with the indicated Weapon. Talents that reference the indicated Weapon may be used in melee.

Hard to Kill

While this model has 2 or more **Wd** remaining when it suffers **Dg,** it may only be reduced to 1 **Wd** by a single damage source.

Hard to Wound

Damage Flips against this model receive one ▭ per indicated number (#).

Harmless

Enemy models must win a **Wp→12** Duel when targeting this model with an attack or the Action immediately fails. **Harmless** ends when this model performs an Action other than the **(1) Walk** or **(1) Pass** Action. Models with the **Terrifying** and **Ruthless** Abilities ignore the **Harmless** Ability.

Hunter

This model ignores cover penalties when targeting models and increases its LoS into and within obscuring terrain to 6".

Immune to Influence

This model is immune to **Wp** Duels when it is the defender.

(+1) Instinctual

This model may perform two different **(0)** Actions during its activation.

Magic Resistant

This model gains **Armor +#** vs. Spells and Spell effects.

(+1) Melee Expert

This model receives one additional specific AP (p.33) during its activation that can only be used for melee **Strike** Actions. This Ability does not stack with Melee Master. This Ability is listed under a model's Actions in its description and on its stat card.

(+2) Melee Master

This model receives two additional specific APs (p.33) during its activation that can only be used for Melee **Strike** Actions. This Ability does not stack with Melee Expert. This Ability is listed under a model's Actions in its description and on its stat card.

(+1) Nimble

This model receives one additional specific AP (p.33) during its activation that can only be used for **Walk** Actions. This Ability is listed under a model's Actions in its description and on its stat card.

Pass Through

This model may move through intervening models but cannot end its movement overlapping another model's base. This model does not ignore disengaging **Strikes** when moving out of an intervening model's melee range.

Poison #

The affected model gains the indicated number (#) of Poison tokens if it has no Poison tokens. If the affected model already has Poison tokens, it replaces them with the indicated number **(#)** if that number is greater than the number of Poison tokens it currently has. The model suffers 1 **Wd** per Poison token on it at the start of its activation, and then discards one Poison token.

(+1) Ranged Expert

This model receives one additional specific AP (p.33) during its activation that can only be used for Ranged **Strike** Actions. This Ability does not stack with Ranged Master. This Ability is listed under a model's Actions in its description and on its stat card.

(+2) Ranged Master

This model receives two additional specific APs (p.33) during its activation that can only be used for Ranged **Strike** Actions. This Ability does not stack with Ranged Expert. This Ability is listed under a model's Actions in its description and on its stat card.

Regeneration

Heal this model the indicated number (#) of **Wd** at the start of its activation.

Ruthless

This model ignores the **Harmless** and **Pitiful** Abilities when targeting enemy models.

Scout

This model ignores severe movement penalties.

Slow to Die

After this model is killed, it may immediately take and resolve a 1 AP Action. This Action's results are applied before the model is removed from play. If the model is healed 1 or more **Wd** while resolving the Action, it is not killed and remains in play.

Terrifying

Living models without **Terrifying** activating, moving through, or ending an Action in this model's melee range, or declaring a **Charge** against this model, must win a Morale Duel or fall back. See p.57 for further details.

Use Soulstones

This model may use game effects that require Soulstones. All Masters and Henchmen automatically have this Ability unless stated otherwise.

COMMON ACTIONS

(2) Flurry

Discard a Control Card. This model immediately makes up to three melee **Strike** Actions against a single target.

(2) Furious Casting

Discard a Control Card. This model receives 3 AP that must immediately be used for **Cast** Actions.

(0) Link

This model and target model in base contact with it are **Linked**. After the model this model is **Linked** to completes a **Walk** Action or ends its activation, Push this model into base contact with the **Linked** model. **Link** ends if the two models are not in base contact at the Start Closing Phase.

(2) Rapid Fire [Weapon]

Discard a Control Card. This model immediately makes up to three ranged **Strike** Actions with this Weapon against a single target.

COMMON TRIGGERS

Ca(🂠🂠) **Surge:** After successfully casting a Spell, discard one Control Card then draw one Control Card.

Cb(🂠) **Brutal [Weapon]:** This Weapon inflicts +1 Dg for each 🂠 in this model's Duel total.

Cb(♣) **Critical Strike [Weapon]:** This Weapon inflicts +1 **Dg** for each ♣ in this model's Duel total. If a weapon is not indicated, the model may use this trigger with any of its melee weapons.

Cb(♥ ♥) **Flay:** When damaging defender with a melee **Strike**, defender suffers +2 **Dg**.

Cb(✕ ✕) **Rot:** When damaging defender with a melee **Strike**, the Damage Flip receives ♠.

GENERAL ACTIONS (available to all models)

(1) Heal: Models with **Use Soulstone** only. Discard 1 Soulstone. This model makes a Healing Flip

(#) Interact: This model spends the indicated number of Actions to Interact with the game table or terrain piece.

(1) Pass: This model does nothing for this Action.

(all) Scavenge: Scavengers Only. This model gains 1 Scrap Counter.

General Movement Actions

(1) Walk: This model moves up to its **Wk** in inches. This may be in any direction and does not need to be in a straight line. A model may **Walk** into melee combat if it chooses (**Severe** terrain costs double to move through. **Impassable** terrain can't be entered. **Climbable** terrain costs 2" per 1 **Ht** up or down. **Hazardous** terrain does damage.).

(2) Charge: This model may take the **Charge** Action if it has a target model within its LoS, which is not already in its melee range. The charging model must move up to its **Cg** in a straight line toward the target, making every effort to end the move with the target in melee range. The model must obey the normal rules for movement including movement penalties and disengaging **Strikes**. At the end of the **Charge** move, if the target is in melee range, the model immediately makes a melee **Strike** with one of its melee Weapons and receives 🌀 on its Damage Flip for that attack. If the target of the Charge is out of melee range at the end of the model's move, the **Charge** Action ends immediately.

(2) Jump: The model can either move 1/2 of its **Wk** distance horizontally and can move over gaps, or the model can move up to 1/2 of its **Wk** distance from a higher elevation to a lower one, or vice versa, without suffering damage.

General Combat Actions

(1) Strike: The model (attacker) targets another model or piece of breakable terrain (defender) within range and performs an opposed Duel using the **Combat (Cb)** value of one of its Weapons against the defender's **Defense (Df)** value, shown as **Cb → Df**. A model must have a melee Weapon to make a melee **Strike** or a ranged Weapon to make a ranged **Strike**.

(1) Defensive Stance: This must be the first Action the model takes during its activation. Until the End Closing Phase, this model's Defense Flips receives 🌀 🌀 when defending in a melee or ranged attack Duel. The model also receives -2/-2 **Wk/Cg** until the End Closing Phase.

(2) Focus: The model performs a melee or ranged **Strike**. The **Strike's** Attack Flip and Damage Flip receive 🌀. Weapons that require more than 1 AP to make a Strike cannot be **Focused**.

General Magic Actions

(#) Cast: This model spends the AP listed before the Spell's name and casts the Spell. Casting a **(0)** Spell counts as a model's **(0)** Action for its activation.

(2) Channel: This model **Casts** a **(1)** Spell. The casting receives 🌀 to both its Casting and any Damage Flips.

(1) Drain Souls: Leaders Only. Sacrifice up to three friendly models within 6", ignoring LoS. The Crew's Soulstone Pool gains one Soulstone for each model sacrificed. Each time a leader takes the **Drain Souls** Action, every non-leader model in the Crew receives a cumulative -1 **Wp** for the remainder of the Encounter. Models with the Insignificant Characteristic cannot be sacrificed by Drain Souls.

Encounter Setup Sequence

1. Choose Encounter Size
2. Choose Factions
3. Choose Encounter Location
4. Choose Deployment Type
5. Determine Strategies
6. Hire Crews
7. Choose Schemes
8. Deploy Crews

ENCOUNTERS

At the end of an Encounter, players reveal all secret Schemes and add up the VP they earned for completing their Strategies and Schemes. When scoring a Strategy or Scheme, score all victory conditions that apply to you. **A player can score a maximum of 8 VP in Scraps and 10 VP in Brawls. Any VP earned beyond the maximum are ignored. The player with the most VP is the winner. If players are tied for VP, the Encounter is a draw.**

Encounter Size

	Scrap	Brawl
Soulstone Range	1-55	30-80
Maximum Control Hand Size per Crew	6	7
Number of Leaders per Crew	1	1-2
Maximum Starting Soulstone Pool Size per Crew	8	10
Total # of Schemes	0-2	0-3
Maximum VP Earned	8	10

Encounter Location

Black Joker	Flipping Player Chooses Location
1-8	Outdoor Location
9-13	Indoor Location
Red Joker	Non-Flipping Player Chooses Location

Encounter Location

	Outdoor	Indoor
Black Joker	Flipping Player Chooses Location	
1	Hag's Territory	Theater
2	Gremlin Village	Sewers
3	Bayou's Edge	Arcanist's Lab
4	Bogs	Resurrectionist's Lab
5	Downtown	Guild Library
6	Industrial Zone	Necropolis
7	Slums	Guild Holding Facility
8	Quarantine Zone	Warehouse
9	Ruins	Research Facility
10	Mine	Cave/Mine System
11	Pioneer/Ghost Town	Ancient Ruins
12	Badlands	Large Tavern
13	Mountains	Collapsed City Block
Red Joker	Non-Flipping Player Chooses Location	

Core Encounter Chart

Jokers	Player Chooses Strategy
1-2	Treasure Hunt
3-5	Destroy the Evidence
6-8	Reconnoiter
9-11	Claim Jump
12-13	Slaughter

Expanded Encounter Chart

Jokers	Flipping Player Chooses Type of Strategy (Individual, Shared, or Story)
1	Story Encounter OR Each Player Flips on the Individual Strategies Chart
2-8	Each Player Flips on the Individual Strategies Chart
9-12	One Player Flips on the Shared Strategy Chart
13	Story Encounter OR One Player Flips on the Shared Strategy Chart

Strategies Chart

	Individual	Shared
Black Joker	Opponent's Choice	
1	A Line in the Sand	Shared A Line in the Sand
2	Claim Jump	Shared Claim Jump
3	Contain Power	Shared Contain Power
4	Deliver a Message	Shared Deliver a Message
5	Destroy the Evidence	Shared Destroy the Evidence
6	Distract	Shared Distract
7	Escape and Survive	Shared Escape and Survive
8	Plant Evidence	Shared Plant Evidence
9	Reconnoiter	Shared Reconnoiter
10	Slaughter	Shared Slaughter
11	Supply Wagon	Shared Supply Wagon
12	Treasure Hunt	Shared Treasure Hunt
13	Turf War	Shared Turf War
Red Joker	Player's Choice	

Deployment Chart

Black Joker	Flipping Player Chooses from the Deployment Areas in the Deployment Chart
1-4	**Diagonal**
	Draw a line between two opposite table corners. Each Crew's Deployment Zone begins 12.5" from that line.
5-9	**Standard**
	Each Deployment Zone comprises a 6" deep section, running the entire length of the table, on opposite table edges.
10-13	**Corners**
	Deployment Areas are 12" x 12" squares in two opposite corners of the table.
Red Joker	Non-Flipping Player Chooses from the Deployment Areas in the Deployment Chart

Varying Encounter Length

A standard Malifaux Encounter lasts 6 turns but may carry on even longer. At the end of turn 6, the player who activated the last model in the turn flips a Fate Card. If the Card value is a 10 or higher, play another turn, but increase the value needed to continue the Encounter on next turn's flip by one. The Encounter ends when the flip is less than the value needed.

Factions and Suits

Faction	Malifaux Suit	Standard Suit	Faction Emblem
Guild	Rams ♙	Hearts ♥	
Resurrectionists	Crows ✗	Spades ♠	
Arcanists	Tomes 📖	Clubs ♣	
Neverborn	Masks 🐾	Diamonds ♦	

Friendly and Enemy Models

Because different game effects can depend on a model's current alliance with its Crew, a model will be friendly to its Crew and an enemy of opposing Crews during an Encounter.

A model is *friendly* when:
- It is under that Crew's Control
- It was hired by a Crew and is currently under that Crew's control.
- It was brought into play by a friendly model and is currently under that Crew's control.

A model is an *enemy* when:
- It is currently under another Crew's control.
- It was hired by another Crew and is currently under that Crew's control.
- It was brought into play by an enemy model and is currently under that Crew's control.

Declaring a Target

When an effect requires a *target*, the following should be determined in order:
- First, check that the item in question is in the targeting model's LoS.
- Then, check for any special situations that may allow or prevent the item to be targeted.
- Finally, check for Talents/Spells that may allow/prevent targeting.

If all of these factors allow the item to be targeted, then the model can declare that item as the target. Measure range to the target. If the target is within the effect's range and meets the above requirements, it is considered a *legal target* of the effect.

Attacks

Attacks can come from multiple sources:
- Attacks with the ⚔ icon are melee attacks, while attacks with the 🏹 icon are ranged attacks
- Spells with a ⚔ / 🏹 icon in their **Rg**
- Spells that require a Resist Duel (see Magic, p.50)
- **Strikes** with melee/ranged Weapons (see Combat, p.39)
- Actions that inflict **Dg** or **Wd** on another model, or require an Opposed Duel.

Bash

All models have access to the melee weapon **Bash** with Rg ⚔ 1, **Cb 3**, and **Dg 0/1/2**, even though it is not listed on their stat card.

Game Effects

Effect is a game term referring to anything that changes a model's state. Some models are able to *ignore* or are *immune* to game effects (X). A model immune to or able to ignore X cannot be affected or modified by X when resolving the effect. Duels requiring X do not occur.

Turn Sequence

1) Draw Phase
- A. Start Draw Phase Step
- B. Discard Control Cards Step
- C. Draw Control Cards Step
- D. End Draw Phase Step

2) Activation Phase
- A. Start Activation Phase Step
- B. Flip for Initiative Step
- C. Alternating Activations Step
- D. End Activation Phase Step

3) Closing Phase
- A. Start Closing Phase Step
- B. Resolve Effects Step
- C. Shuffle Fate Decks Step
- D. End Closing Phase Step

Performing a Duel

1. Flip for Starting Duel Total.
2. Change Starting Total or Pass.
   - a. Cheat Fate
   - b. Use Soulstones
3. Determine Final Duel Total.
4. Declare Trigger.
5. Determine Success.
6. Apply Duel Results

Strike Attack Sequence

1. Declare Target, then Check Range
2. Strike Duel
   - a. Flip Starting Attack and Defense Totals
   - b. Change Starting Totals or Pass
   - c. Determine Final Duel Totals
   - d. Declare Triggers
   - e. Determine Success
   - f. Apply Duel Results

Casting Sequence

1. Declare Spell and Target
2. Casting Duel
   - a. Caster Flips Starting Casting Total
   - b. Caster Changes Starting Total or Passes
   - c. Caster Determines Final Duel Total
   - d. Caster Declares a Trigger
   - e. Caster Determines Success
3. Resist Duels (if necessary)
   - a. Resisting Model Flips Starting Resist Total
   - b. Resisting Model Changes Starting Total or Passes
   - c. Resisting Model Determines Final Duel Total
   - d. Caster Meets Additional Requirements
   - e. Resisting Model Declares a Trigger
   - f. Resisting Model Determines Success
4. Apply Spell Effects

Fate Modifiers

- Combine all modifiers for flip (ex. 🔼🔼 and 🔽 = 🔼 modifier).
- One or more 🔼: flip one card plus one card per 🔼 and choose the card.
- One or more 🔽: flip one card plus one card per 🔽 and take the lowest value card (tie, player chooses).
- Cannot Cheat Fate if one or more 🔽 exist for the flip.
- Maximum of three 🔼's or 🔽's in any flip.

Jokers

- Flip/play Black Joker: value 0 and no suit. Must be chosen over any other card, including the Red Joker.
- Flip/play Red Joker: value 14 and choose suit. Can be chosen in a 🔽 flip over lowest card.

Combat Total Modifier Chart

If the combat total was...	0	1-5	6-10	11+
The attacker's Damage Flip receives...	⊟ ⊟	⊟	No modifier	⊞

Damage Chart

If the value of the flip is...	Black Joker	1-5	6-10	11+	Red Joker
The damage is...	No Damage	Weak	Moderate	Severe	Severe + another Damage Flip

Healing Chart

If the value of the flip is...	Black Joker	1-5	6-10	11+	Red Joker
The # of **Wd** healed is...	Nothing	1	2	3	Heal all **Wd**

Wound Prevention Chart

If the value of the flip is...	Black Joker	1-5	6-10	11+	Red Joker
The # of **Wd** prevented is...	Nothing	1	2	3	All Incoming **Wd**

Action Modifiers

- **(+1) Fast:** This model receives 1 additional general AP during its current or next activation, whichever comes first.
- **(-1) Slow:** This model forfeits 1 general AP during its current or next activation, whichever comes first.
- **Paralyzed:** A model gaining **Paralyzed** during its activation loses any remaining AP and its activation immediately ends. If the model gains **Paralyzed** outside of its activation, it forfeits its next activation. While **Paralyzed,** a model has no melee range, cannot take any type of Action, cannot activate Triggers, and cannot react to disengaging models. A **Paralyzed** model does not make a fall back move when it loses a Morale Duel, but does rally as normal (Morale, p.56).
- **Reactivate:** This model may activate a second time this turn during the normal activation sequence. A model may only activate a second time through **Reactivate** once per turn.